Python for Data Analysis

Master Deep Learning with Python Language and Become Great at Programming Python for Beginners with Hands-on Project (Data Science)

Jason Scratch

Table of Contents

Introduction

Congratulations on purchasing *Python for Data Analysis* and thank you for doing so.

The following chapters will discuss everything that we need to know when it comes to deep learning and a good data analysis. Many companies are shifting the way they do things. Collecting data has become the norm, and now they have to learn what is inside all of that data, and what insights they can learn in the process. And this is exactly what a data analysis can help them to do. With a bit of the Python language, an understanding of deep learning, and some of the best deep learning libraries available we can create our own models and put that data to work.

To start this guidebook, we are going to take a look at some of the basics of deep learning and what data analysis is all about. There are a lot of buzz words out there when it comes to machine learning and artificial intelligence, and understanding how these two topics can fit into the mix is so important for ensuring that we will get things done.

From there, we will move a bit into Python and how it fits into this process. We will start this with some information on the best libraries form Python that help with deep learning before moving on to how we can work with some of the different types of neural networks you can create. This section is also a great one to explore to learn more about some of the Python deep learning libraries you can use including TensorFlow, Keras, and PyTorch and how these can help us create some of the models that we want within the field of deep learning and data analysis.

To end this guidebook, we will take a look at machine learning and how this process can fit in with the other topics we have discussed, especially when we look at deep learning. And then we end with a discussion on how deep learning can help businesses with their own predictive analysis. This makes it easier for companies to make data-based business decisions to help them get ahead on the market.

A data analysis is an important part of any business, especially those who have spent a lot of time collecting big data. But doing this in the right manner can be critical to ensure we get accurate insights and predictions. When you are ready to learn more

There are plenty of books on this subject on the market, thanks again for choosing this one! Every effort was made to ensure it is full of as much useful information as possible, please enjoy!

Chapter 1:

What Is Deep Learning?

The world of data science and the various terms and processes that go with it has really taken off steam. Many companies have started to realize that they can use this information and the fact that computers and systems are able to train themselves, for their own advantage, and they are excited to learn more about how to make this happen.

No matter what industry you are in, processes like data analysis, machine learning, artificial intelligence, and deep learning can come into play and provide you with some great results in the process. But with this in mind, we are going to spend some time focusing on deep learning and what it is able to do for your business.

Deep learning is a process that can carry out what we need with the world of machine learning, often using an artificial neural net that is composed of a lot of levels arranged in a type of hierarchy to make things easier. The network is going to learn something simple when you enter into the first level, and then it will work to send that information, and everything that it has learned in that part, over to the next level.

From here, the next level is able to take some of this simple information and will try to combine it together with something that is seen as a bit more complex, before passing all of that over to the third level. This is a process that will just continue from one level to the next, with each level building something that is more complex from any input that it received with the previous level.

This is an interesting process that shows us exactly how deep learning is meant to work, and why it is so valuable. It is basically a process where the computer is able to teach itself how to learn, based on a simple program that a data scientist is able to add to the system. It is that easy! We will talk about some of the best libraries and the best algorithms from machine learning and deep learning to make this happen, but having a good understanding of how it all works can really make a difference in how you are able to use it.

What Is Deep Learning

The first topic that we need to dive into here is what deep learning is all about. Deep learning is considered a function that comes with artificial intelligence, one that is able to imitate, as closely as possible, some of the workings we see in the human brain when it comes to creating patterns and processing complex data to use with decision making. Basically, we can use the parts of deep learning to help us take our machine or our system and teach it how to think through things the same way that a human can, although at a faster and more efficient rate.

Deep learning is going to be considered a subset of machine learning, which is also a subset of artificial intelligence. It also has a network that is capable of learning a lot from data that is unsupervised, along with data that is unlabeled or unstructured. There are other names for this kind of learning as well including deep neural network and deep neural learning.

So, to get a better idea of how this is going to benefit us, we first need to take a look at how we can work with deep learning. The process of deep learning has really evolved a lot in the past few years, going hand in hand with a lot of the things we have seen in the digital era. This time period has really brought about so much data, data that comes in so many forms. In particular, this data is known as big data, and we will be able to draw it out of a lot of different areas such as e-commerce platforms, search engines, social media, and more.

If a company uses some of the algorithms that come with machine learning, they will be able to actually use all of the information that they are collecting. They can use it to recommend products for their customers, to really work on making predictions and finding patterns with the information so they can really run their business the way that they would like.

You will notice though that this unstructured data is going to be pretty large, and for an employee to go through this information and get the relevant parts from it, it would take so long the information would no longer be relevant and useful. And by the time they did, the information would be old, and the world would have already moved on and presented different information. But many companies still realized the potential that they could learn from all of this information, even if it is pretty large, and many are looking at the different ways that various systems of AI can help them get through this information and gain the insights that they need.

With this in mind, it is important that we take some time to look at how deep learning is going to work. Deep learning has evolved at the same time and often at the same pace as we see with the digital era. This is an era that has seen a big explosion of data in all forms, and from every region of the world. This is a lot of data, and it is there to help businesses make informed decisions that weren't possible in the past.

Think about all of the information that you already have at your fingertips, and you may not even realize that it is there. Before you even decide to start working with big data, you already know that if you need to look up something, you can head to your favorite search engine and it will all be there. Our digital era is bringing out a ton of new information and data, and the smart companies, the ones who would like to get ahead, are the ones who not only gather all of that data, but who learn how to use it.

This data, which is often called big data, is drawn from a variety of sources depending on what the business is trying to accomplish. these can come from places like e-commerce platforms, search engines, online cinemas, search engines, and more. The enormous amount of data that fits into the category of big data is going to be readily accessible to anyone who wants it, and it is possible to share it through a lot of different applications like cloud computing.

However, this data, which is normally going to come to us in a form that is unstructured, is so vast that if a person manually went through all of it, it may take decades to extract out the information that is relevant to what they need. Companies realize this, and they now that there is a lot of potential that can be found in all of that data that they have collected. And this is why creating and adapting artificial intelligence systems with automated support is something that many of them have started to focus their attention on.

How Is Deep Learning Different from Machine Learning?

The next thing that we need to focus on in this chapter is the idea of deep learning and machine learning. To someone who hasn't had much of a chance to explore these topics and some of the processes that come with them, these two terms are going to seem like they are identical and that we can use them in an interchangeable manner. But in this section, we are going to explore these a bit more and see how they are similar and how they are different.

One of the most common techniques in artificial intelligence that can be used to help us process some of that big data we have been collecting for a long time is known as machine learning. Machine learning is going to be an algorithm that is self-adaptive. This means that it is able to learn from what has happened in the past and can work on making increasingly better analysis and patterns with data that is newly added over time, and even with some of its own experiences.

There are a lot of examples of how this would be able to work in the real world, and there are a lot of companies who already work to make this happen for their needs. Let's say that we take a look at a company that handles digital payments. One of their main concerns is to keep the levels of potential and actual fraud from occurring in the system. Instances of fraud can cost them millions of dollars a year, if not more, and being able to catch these ahead of time and understanding how to prevent these before they happen could be a lifesaver for most of these financial companies.

The good news is that these digital payment companies could employ some tools of machine learning for this kind of purpose. The computational algorithm that would be added into your computer model will work to process all of the transactions that happen on our digital platform and can make sure that we find the right patterns in any set of data. If it has been able to learn in the right manner, the algorithm will be able to point out any anomaly and more that is detected in this pattern.

Deep learning, which is a subset of machine learning, can work in a similar manner, but it does this in a more specific way and includes specific machine learning algorithms to get things done. When we talk about the deep learning process, we are looking at a form of machine learning that will utilize a hierarchical level of artificial neural networks in order to make sure that the process of machine learning is carried out properly.

These artificial neural networks are going to be built up much like the human brain, and there are nodes of neurons that will connect with one another similar to a web. These nodes are able to send information to each other and will communicate with one another to make this process work well.

Unlike some of the traditional programs that are going to work in a linear way to build up a new analysis with the data at hand, the hierarchical function that comes with a system of deep learning is going to enable our machines and any systems that we use with this process to go through the data with an approach that is more nonlinear.

Let's go back a bit to that example that we did with fraud protection with an online payment company. If this company worked with a more traditional approach to detecting things like money laundering and fraud they would rely on the system just picking up on the amount of the transaction. This means that they would only catch the issues when there was a large amount of money taken out, and maybe a few times if there was a really strange location that didn't make sense to where the person was located. We can see where this can run into some troubles because not every instance of fraud or money laundering is going to include big amounts, and most people who try to do these tasks are going to stick with smaller amounts to stay under the radar.

But when we work with deep learning, we are able to work with a technique that is seen as nonlinear, and this would include things like the time of the transaction, the type of retailer that is being used, the IP address, the geographic location of the user and when the transaction happens, and any other features that the company would like to rely on, in order to point out when a transaction is likely to be fraudulent.

The first layer that comes with this process of the neural network is that we will take the raw data and input it. This could include something like the amount of the transaction. Then this is turned over as the output of that first layer. The second layer will use that output to work on itself, and may include some additional information like the IP address, and will pass all of this as its results or output as well.

Then we move on to the third layer. This layer is going to take all of the information from the second layer, and includes some more raw data, like the geographic location, and will make the pattern of the machine even better from here. This will continue on through all of the layers that the programmer set up with the neural network until the system can determine whether the transaction is legitimate or fraudulent.

Remember here that deep learning is going to be considered a function of artificial intelligence that helps us to mimic the workings of what happens inside the human brain, at least when it comes to processing through a lot of data to make important decisions. Deep learning with artificial intelligence can be useful because it can learn from the data, whether we have data that is labeled, or if we are working with data that is both unlabeled and unstructured. Deep learning, which is a subset of the popular machine learning, can be used to help out almost any industry that we can think of, but in the example that we talked about above, it is especially helpful with detecting things like fraud and the laundering of money.

One Example of How Deep Learning Works

The next thing that we need to focus on is how deep learning works. And the best way to really see how this kind of technology is going to benefit us and give us some of the results we want is by taking a look at some of the examples of it in action.

If we stick with that system of fraud detection that we worked on before with machine learning, it is possible to create an example of deep learning in no time. if the system for machine learning was able to create a model with parameters built around the number of dollars a user is able to receive or send, the method of deep learning can start to build on some of the results that are offered through machine learning.

Each layer that comes with this neural network is able to work because it helps to build-up on the previous layer. And with each of these layers, we are going to be able to add on some important data, like the IP address, credit score, the retailer and the sender, a social media event, the user, and even a credit score based on what needs to happen with the data and the machine.

The algorithms that come with deep learning are going to be trained not just to create some patterns from the transactions, but they will also let us know when a pattern is signaling that there is a need for someone to come in and investigate activity that may seem fraudulent. The final layer of this is going to relay a signal over to the analyst, who can then choose to freeze the account in question until the investigation is completed and they determine whether or not money laundering is happening.

It is possible to work with deep learning across all industries with a number of tasks based on what those industries need to accomplish. some commercial apps, for example, are able to use this technology to help out with things like image recognition. There are open-source platforms that come with consumer recommendation apps and even some medical research tools that explore the possibility of reusing drugs for new ailments. These are just a few examples of what we are able to see when we add in deep learning and some of the algorithms that come with this type of learning.

Why Does Deep Learning Matter?

Another thing that we need to explore a bit here is why deep learning is going to matter so much? And why is this form of machine learning able to help us attain such impressive results where other methods may fail? To make it simple, deep learning works due to accuracy. The algorithms with deep learning are able to achieve recognition accuracy at levels that are much higher than was possible before.

This is helpful because it helps any consumer electronics meet the expectations of the user, and it is so crucial when it comes to applications that rely on safety such as the recent development of driverless cars. Some of the recent advances in deep learning have been able to step up and improved to the point wherein many cases, the systems that rely on deep learning are actually able to outperform what a human can do manually in several tasks, such as classifying the objects found I images.

While the idea of deep learning has been around for a number of years and was first theorized in the 1980s, there are two big reasons why we are just hearing about it today, and why it wasn't really seen as something useful to work with in the past.

These two reasons include:

1. To get the most out of deep learning, we needed to have a large amount of labeled data. Getting this data is expensive, especially when it comes to the large amounts that were needed to get this to run.

2. Another issue is that deep learning requires us to have quite a bit of computing power. High-performance GPUs have a parallel architecture that is the most efficient when it comes to deep learning. When we combine them with things like cloud computing or clusters, this is going to enable the teams to reduce their time for training this network. They can get it done in a few hours, rather than in a few weeks.

How Does This Deep Learning Work?

To really understand this deep learning, we need to take this further and see how it works. Most of the methods that we want to use with deep learning are going to rely on the architecture of a neural network, which is why we often refer to these models as deep neural networks. The term deep is there because it will refer back to the number of hidden layers that show up in the neural network. Traditional neural networks that you can create with machine learning are just going to work with two or three hidden layers in most cases, but deep networks can go up to 150, and it is likely this number will grow over time.

The models of deep learning are trained because they rely on large sets of data that are labeled, along with architectures of neural networks. These are able to come together to learn features directly without the need for extraction of the features manually.

While there are a few different types of deep neural networks that a programmer is able to focus on, one of the best options, and the one that data scientists are the most likely to use, is the convolutional neural network, or CNN. A CNN is going to convolve together the features that are learned with the data you've add-in, and then uses the 2D convolutional layers, which will make this architecture well suited when it is time to process any 2D data, including options like images.

CNN's are nice for a number of reasons, but they also help with eliminating the need for manual feature extraction. What this means is that we do not need to go through and identify features that are used to help classify the images. CNN is going to work by extracting features right out of the image. The relevant features will not be trained ahead of time because they will be learned while the network is training on a collection of images that you provide as we go.

This may sound complicated, but when we add in the automated feature extraction to the mix, it is going to make things easier. It will ensure that the models you make with deep learning end up being really accurate for a variety of computer vision tasks, including object classification.

CNN's are able to learn how to detect a variety of features that come within an image, using what could be tens of thousands of hidden layers in the process. Every hidden layer is going to increase the complexity that comes with the learned image features. An example of this would be that the first hidden layer is going to be responsible for detecting the edges of the image, and then the last layer, however many that will be, will work on detecting some of the more complex shapes that will help it to figure out what objects are in that specific image.

Creating and Training Our Deep Learning Models

We will take more time to get in-depth about this in a bit, but we are going to take a moment to look at some of the basics that come into play when we want to create and then train some of our own deep learning models. There are three methods that are pretty common to work with, especially when we want to focus on object classification including:

Training from scratch. To work on training our own deep network from scratch, we have to take on a few big steps that can take some time. First, we need to gather up a large amount of data, specifically a large labeled data set. Then we have to design the architecture that we need for the network, ensuring that it is going to be able to learn the features that are found in that labeled set of data, and that it can model it as well.

This is a very time-consuming option to work with, but it can be good when we want to create a brand-new application, or if we are working with an application that has a large number of output categories. Of course, because of the amount of data that we need, especially considering that it is a large amount of labeled data, and the rate of learning, this is the least common out of all the approaches. Usually, they will take weeks or longer to properly train, but they can still be a good option in some cases.

Then we can work with what is known as transfer learning. Most of the applications that you see with deep learning will work on the transfer learning approach. This is a process that will have us working on a pre-trained model and then fine-tuning some of the parts.

To make this one work, we want to pick out a network that already exists, such as GoogLeNet or AlexNet and then feed in some new data that contains classes that were previously unknown. After we make the necessary changes and tweaks to the network, we are now able to perform the new task, such as categorizing just dogs or cats, instead of focusing on 1000 different objects at a time.

This kind of model for deep learning is going to have a few advantages, but one of these benefits is that it needs much less data to complete. We can limit the processing to just a few thousand images, rather than focusing on millions of images like the network may have done in the beginning. This allows the computation costs and time to drop, often getting the model done in a few minutes depending on the situation.

This kind of learning is going to require us to have an interface to the internals of the pre-existing network, so it can be modified and enhanced in a more surgical manner to handle the new tasks that you set out. MATLAB has all of the functions and the tools that you need to make sure that you see the best results with transfer learning.

And the third option that we can work with when it comes to creating a deep learning model is feature extraction. A slightly less common method, mostly because it is more of a specialized approach that can work with deep learning, is to use our network as a feature extractor. Considering that all of our layers are going to have the responsibility of learning certain features from an image, we are able to pull these features out of the network at any time that we want during our training process. These are the features that we can then utilize in a variety of different models, including SVM or support vector machines, and machine learning models of other kinds as well.

However, you may find that training one of these models for deep learning can take up a lot of time, sometimes days and even weeks. This doesn't mean that they aren't worth the time and the effort that you put in, but sometimes a business wants to be able to take all of the data they have and create a good model to work with right away, rather than having to wait days or weeks to even get started.

When we work with something known as GPU acceleration, it is able to provide us with a significant increase in this process. When we use the MATLAB with GPU, it is able to reduce the amount of time that it takes to train a network, and can cut the training time for an image classification problem from days to just hours. Think about how much faster this can be! We can turn on one of our deep learning models with these tools within one working day, and get amazing results with deep learning if we use it the right way.

Don't worry if you are not completely familiar with the GPUs and how they work. MATLAB is going to use the GPU, whenever it is available, without requiring us to understand how to program with these GPUs explicitly. This makes the whole process a bit easier to handle.

There is just so much that we are able to do when it comes to deep learning. This is a process that comes with machine learning, so as you get started, it is easy to get the two terms mixed up and a bit confused. But with some of the lessons that we will take a look at in this guidebook, we can gather a better understanding of deep learning and what it is able to do for us.

Chapter 2:

What Is a Data Analysis?

While we are on the topic of deep learning, we need to take some time to dive into another topic that is closely related. When we were talking about deep learning a bit above, we mentioned quite a bit about data, and how this data is meant to help train and test the models that we try to make with the use of deep learning. In this chapter, we are going to talk about data analytics, which is the process of not only gathering the data but sorting through that data and finding what predictions, insights, and information is inside.

A data analysis can happen in many different ways. But since most of these analyses are done on large sets of data, also known as big data, it is hard for a human to manually go through all of that information and learn what is inside, especially in a timely manner. This is where deep learning comes into the mix and helps us to do a good analysis in no time. With that in mind, let's dive in a bit and take a closer look at what data analysis is all about.

What Is a Data Analysis?

There is a ton of data that is available in our world. Companies like to spend time collecting information from their customers, data from their social media accounts, and data from other sources in their industry. This data is going to help them to really get a competitive edge if they use it the right way and can ensure that they release the right products while providing good customer service in the process.

The problem is that after you collect your data, you then have to be able to go through all of that data. This is not an easy thing to do all of the time. There is often a ton of data, and figuring out how to go through it, and what information is found inside the data is going to be hard. Gathering all of the data that you need and then not following through and analyzing it is such a waste, and you might as well save time and not go through with this at all. But if you have gathered the data, we need to be able to go through and analyze the data in order to make smarter business decisions. And that is what we are going to spend time on in this guidebook.

Data analysis is going to be a practice of a company where they take the raw data and then order and organize it out in a manner that we are able to look through all of the useful information that is in there is extracted out to be used. The process of organizing and then be able to think about the data is going to be the key to understanding what the data does, and what it doesn't, contain. There can be a lot of data that the company provides you, but if you are not able to go through it and see what information is inside of it, then the data is not going to help you, and you will have no idea what is inside the data, and what is not inside of the data.

Now, when we are working with data analysis, there are going to be quite a few methods that we can add in here in order to handle the analysis, and make sure that we will see some results. However, no matter what method you choose to go with, there has to be some caution with how we want to manipulate the data. We don't want to end up pushing our own agendas and conclusions on the data. We want to see the actual insights and information that are found inside of all that data.

Yes, you will go through this process with some questions that you want answered, and maybe also a hypothesis about what you are going to find in the data. But if you are careful, you will not open up your mind to all of the information that is found in that data, and you will miss out on valuable insights and predictions that your business needs. And how much worth or value will we assign to the data if we end up analyzing it in the wrong manner in the first place? Our whole goal here is to find out what is in the information, and learn what the data can actually tell us, without our own biases in the process.

If you are going to ignore this advice, and just dive in with your own conclusions and without paying attention to what the data is actually trying to tell you, then you may as well give up right now. You will find exactly what you want, but that doesn't mean that we looked at the information in the right manner. And often this steers you, and your business, down the wrong path.

The first thing that we need to take a look at here is what data analysis is all about. When we look at data analytics, we see that it is the science used to analyze lots of raw data to help a company make smart and informed conclusions and decisions about that information. Many of the techniques and the processes that come with data analytics have been automated into mechanical processes and algorithms that are able to work the raw data over in a manner that makes it easier for humans to learn from.

This process is much easier to complete, and much faster, than having someone manually go through and read that information. This makes it easier for companies to use all of that big data they have been collecting. You can have all of the big data that you want, and you can store it in any manner that you would like, but if that data is never analyzed and read through, you will find that it is basically useless.

The techniques that are available for us to use with data analysis are going to be helpful in that they reveal trends and metrics that would otherwise get really lost in the mass of information. Remember that companies have learned the value of lots of data and this means that while they are collecting all of that data they could easily lose out on some of the insights because it gets hidden inside with all of the noise.

Once the company is able to use a model of deep learning to help with a good data analysis, and they figure out what the metrics and trends for that information entails, they can then use this information to optimize the processes that will help increase the overall efficiency that we see in that system, and maybe even for the whole company.

To make this a bit further, we have to understand that data analytics is a very broad term that is able to encompass a lot of diverse types of data analysis at some point. Any type of information that you have collected and perhaps stored can be subjected to the techniques of data analytics if you want to see what is in a group of information to use it to further your business and to beat out the competition, then it doesn't matter what kind of information you have, the data analyst can still find the insights that will improve your business.

For example, we may find that many manufacturing companies are going to work with a data analysis to help them run and perform better. For example, they may record the runtime, the amount of downtime, and then the work queue, or how long it takes the system to do a specific item, for various machines. They can then analyze all of this information and data to make it easier to plan out the workloads, ensuring that each machine is operating closer to the peak capacity that it can during working hours.

Data analytics can help us to make sure that there are no longer any bottlenecks when it comes to production, but this is not the only place where a good data analysis is able to shine. For example, we can see that gaming companies are often going to work with a form of data analytics to ensure that they can reward their players on a set schedule, in a manner that makes it more likely that the majority of the users will remain active in the game, rather than giving up and getting frustrated.

Another example of how this data analysis can work, especially with the right deep learning model, is with the world of content companies. Many of these are already relying on data analytics to keep their customers clicking, re-organizing, or watching content. The more that they can get these clicks and views, the more money they are able to generate from advertisements and such on their website, so they come up with content, headings, and more that keep readers there for as long as possible.

Now, the steps that come with doing a data analysis can be quite involved and take some time to get through. But we are going to focus on some of the basics that come with each step, so that we can get a good general idea of how this process is meant to work, and why so many businesses are able to see some great results when they use a data analysis on their own data:

1. The first thing that we need to do is make a determination of the requirements we want to place on the data, or how we would like to group our data. Data may be separated out in any manner that you would like including by gender, income, demographics, and age. And the values of the data can be numerical, or we can divide them out by category. Knowing your business problem and what you are hoping to solve with this data analysis can make it easier to know exactly what the requirements of the data should be.

2. The next step that we need to focus on here is to collect the data. Without any data, we are not going to be able to create the deep learning models that we want, and we will be stuck without any analysis at all. We are able to collect the data from a variety of sources, including from computers, online sources, cameras and through personnel, and environmental sources.

3. Once we have been able to collect the data that we want to use, it is time to go through a few steps in order to organize that data. This makes it easier to analyze the data without mistakes or errors showing up. Organization may take some time and the method that you use will depend on the type of data and what you are trying to learn.

4. While you are organizing the data, we need to also take some time to clean it up. This means that we want the data scrubbed and then checked to make sure that there are no duplications or errors that will be there and that the data is not incomplete in any manner. This is a good step to work with because it will fix up any of the errors in the set of data before you try to move the data along and perform your analysis on it.

The Data Analytics Process

The application of data analytics is going to involve a few different steps, rather than just analyzing the data that you have gathered, particularly on some of the more advanced projects of analysis, much of the required work is going to take place up front, such as with collecting, integrating, and preparing data. Then we can move on to the part where we develop, test, and review the analytical models that we have to ensure that they are producing results that are accurate.

The analytics process is going to start from the very beginning, where we work on collecting data. This is where the data scientist and their team will identify the information that they need to find and gather for a particular analytics application, and then they will continue to work on their own, or with some IT staffers and data engineers to assemble all of that gathered data for human consumption.

Data from different sources can sometimes be combined, with the help of a data integration routine, transformed into a common format, and then loaded up into what is known as an analytics system. There are a number of these systems available for you to choose from including a data warehouse, NoSQL database, and a Hadoop cluster.

In some other situations, the collection process is going to be a bit different. In this case, the collection process could consist of pulling the relevant subset out of a stream of raw data that flows into your storage, and then moving it over to a second, and separate, partition in the system. This can be done in order to allow for an analysis of the information, without any of the work that you do affect the set of data overall.

Once we have been able to gather up the data that we need and we have gotten it into place, the next step that we need to work on is to find and then fix any of the quality problems that are in the data. We want to clean up any of the quality problems that could potentially affect the accuracy of our applications as we go along. This can include a number of different processes including data cleansing and data profiling to ensure that the information in our set of data is as consistent as possible, and that the duplicate entries and errors can be eliminated.

In addition to what we have been able to do so far, there is some additional work for data preparation that we need to focus on. This work is important because it is going to manipulate and organize the data that you plan to use in the analysis. You should add in some policies of data governance in order to help the data stay within the standards of your company, and that everything is done according to industry standards.

When you reach this point, the process of data analytics is going to get started in earnest. The data scientist is going to build up an analytical model working with some tools of predictive modeling or analytics software. There are a number of programming languages that we are able to focus on as well, including SQL, R, Scala, and Python, to get the work done. The model is initially going to be run against a partial set of data because this is one of the best ways to check out the amount of accuracy that is present in that model.

Of course, the first test is not going to be as accurate as you would like, which means that the data scientist has to revise the model as needed and test again. This is a process that is known as training the model, and we continue working with it until get can get all of the parts together, and the model functions as we intended.

Finally, we are going to run the model on what is known as the production model. This means that the model is going to be run against the full set of data. This is going to be done once because it is going to help us address a specific need in information. Then there are times when it is going to be done on an ongoing basis, any time that we update the data.

In some cases, the applications of the analytics can be set up in a manner that will trigger business actions automatically. For example, we may see this happen with some of the stock trades that a financial services firm is going to use. Otherwise, the last step of this process of data analytics is communicating the results generated by the analytical models that you used to business executives and other end-users to aid in how they make their important decisions.

There are a few different methods that you can use to make this happen, but the most common technique to work with here is data visualization. What this means is that the data scientist and any team they are working with will take the information they gathered out of the model, and then turn this into a chart or another type of infographic. This is done to help make it easier to understand the findings

One more thing that we need to take a look at here is that we have to consider the variety of statistical methods that we have available with our data analysis, and then decide how we can use each one. There are a few that are really good at getting this done, but often it will depend on what we would like to accomplish with all of this. But first, we need to take a look at them and how they will be able to help us get the results that we want.

Some of the best statistical methods that you may want to consider for your project will include:

1. The general linear model. This is going to be a generalization of the linear regression to the case of having two or more of the dependent variables that you need to rely on.

2. Generalized linear model. This one may sound like the other model, but it is a bit different. It is going to be an extension and works best when your dependent variables are more discrete.

3. Structural equation modeling. This particular type of modeling is going to be usable when you would like to assess some of the latent structures that were measured from your manifest variables.

4. Item response theory: With these types of models, they are going to be used to help us asses just one of the variables that are latent from the variables that are binary measured.

Depending on the kind of information that you have present, and what your final goal in the process is, there are a few different approaches that you are able to use in order to help get the data analysis done.

Some of the most common ones that you can choose from (and again, look to your data and what you are trying to figure out from that information to help make the decision), are going to include the following:

1. Cross-cultural analysis
2. Content analysis
3. Grounded theory analysis
4. Discourse analysis
5. Hermeneutic analysis
6. Constant comparative analysis
7. Phenomenological analysis
8. Narrative analysis
9. Ethnographic analysis

Why Does Data Analytics Matter?

While we are here, we need to take a few minutes to discuss why data analytics is so important, and why so many businesses are jumping on board with this in the hopes of seeing some improvements along the way. the reason that data analytics is so important is because it can help a business to optimize their performances overall.

When the company is able to implement the data analysis into their business model, it means that they are able to reduce the costs that they experience on a day to day basis. This happens because the analysis will help them to identify the best, and the most efficient, ways of doing business, and because they are able to store up large amounts of data to help them get all of this process done in a timely manner.

Another benefit of using this data analytics, and why it really does matter for a lot of companies, is that the company can use this process in order to make the best business decisions. These business decisions no longer need to rely on what other companies are doing or on the intuition of key decision-makers. Instead, they rely on the facts and insights provided in the collected data.

Many companies also like to work with the process of data analytics because it will help them learn more about and serve their customers better. Data analytics can help us to analyze customer trends and the satisfaction levels of our customers, which can help the company come up with new, and better, services and products to offer.

The Types of Data Analytics Available

When we take a look at the process of data analytics, we will find that there are a few different types that a company can choose from to get their work done and to really learn what is hidden inside all of that data they have been collecting. To keep it simple, we are going to focus on the four basic types of data analytics that many companies are going to rely on.

First, we have what is known as descriptive analytics. This is the type of data analytics that will describe to us what happens over a given period of time. We may use this one when we want to see whether or not the sales have been stronger this month compared to last month. Or we can use it on our social media pages to figure out whether the number of views that we have received on posts has gone up, down, or remained the same.

Then the second type of data analytics that we can work with is called the diagnostic analytics. This one is a bit different because it will focus more on the why, rather than the what, of something happening. This will involve some data inputs that are a bit more diverse, and the data scientist has to come in here with a bit of hypothesizing ready to go. For example, the data scientist may focus on whether or not the last marketing campaign that was sent out actually impacted sales in a positive or negative manner before prolonging or canceling that marketing.

We can also work with what is known as predictive analytics. This one is going to move us over to what is the most likely thing to happen in the near term. We may ask questions with this one like What happened to sales the last time we had a hot summer? How many of the various models on weather that we have looked at predicting that this summer is going to be a hot one.

And finally, the fourth type of data analytics that we can focus on is going to be known as the prescriptive analytics. This is the type of analytics that is able to suggest a course of action. if we look at the example above, we would take some time to check out how hot the summer is likely to be. When we see that the likelihood of a hot summer is measured as an average of five models of weather, and they predict that the hot summer is 58 percent likely to happen, then you would make some changes to accommodate.

Let's say that when the weather gets hot in the summer, you sell more of your product. Since we have a good estimate from a few different sources, that the weather is going to be hot, we would want to plan accordingly. Maybe you will hire more people, add on some extra shifts, or stock up on your inventory to make sure that you don't run out.

At its core, data analytics is going to underpin some of the quality control systems that show up in the world of finances, including the program known as Six Sigma. If you are in business, it is likely that you have spent at least a bit of time working with Six sigma and all that it entails.

The idea that comes with this Six Sigma program is that a company wants to learn how to cut out waste in any manner possible. The choices they may to do this will depend on their business model, what they hold most dear, and what needs the most work. One company may need to work on reducing the amount of returns that they get from customers, and another may need to find a way to limit the number of steps that are taken to complete the process of creating the product.

The goal with Six Sigma is to slowly but surely cut out the waste and help the company reach near perfection as much as possible. And while these two topics, that of deep learning and Six Sigma, are not topics that most people are going to associate with one another, they can really work hand in hand to make sure that the goals of each can be met.

The main idea that comes with both of these processes though is that if you don't take the time to measure something out properly, whether you are looking at your own weight or another personal measurement, or the number of defects, per million, that happen on the production line, how can you ever hope to optimize the results? This is what deep learning can help us to get done if we just learn how to use it.

Is Anyone Really Using Data Science?

Another question that a lot of people have when it comes to data science and data analysis is whether there are other companies or other industries that are using this kind of technology. Sometimes, with all of the work, the algorithms, and the various programs, it seems like using data science and data analysis is just too much work to handle. But you may be surprised that there are a number of industries and companies out there who are already working with data science, and a data analysis that comes with it, to help them really gain a competitive advantage.

A good example of where this is being used is in the industry of traveling and hospitality. Both of these rely on a quick turnaround to make as much profit as possible, and to ensure that they are not turning guests away all of the time. The good news for this industry is that they are able to collect a ton of data on the customer in order to find any of the problems they need to worry about, which makes it much easier to actually fix the issue.

Another place where we are going to see a lot of data analysis in the healthcare industry. There are so many areas of this industry that can use a good data analysis, especially when it is combined together with machine learning and deep learning, to make doctors and other medical professionals better at their jobs. It can help doctors to look through images and diagnose patients faster, it can help to keep up with the patient and ensure that they are getting the right treatment, it can be used on the floor to monitor the patient and alert nursing staff when something is wrong, and even can help as receptionists and other similar roles when no one else is available to take this job.

And finally, the retail industry is able to benefit from the use of data science in many ways. This is because the companies that fit into this industry are going to use copious amounts of data in order to help them keep up with the demands of the shopper, even though these demands can change over time. the information that is collected and analyzed by retailers will come in use when it is time to identify big trends, recommend products, and increase the amount of profit the company makes.

As we can see here, there are a lot of different parts that come into play when we want to work with a data analysis. It is a pretty easy concept, but one that takes some time and effort in order to see the best results. But when we can take all of the data that we collect over time, and then actually perform an analysis on the information to gather some good insights and predictions to make smarter business decisions, we will find that data analysis can be well worth our time.

Chapter 3:

The Python Libraries for Deep Learning

S o, at this point, we have talked a lot about deep learning and data analysis, and now it is time to take some of that information, and put it to good use. You are probably interested in deep learning, and maybe even in making some of your own Convolutional Neural Networks, but are wondering where you should start. The best step is to pick out the library that you want to use. But this brings up another challenge because there are just so many coding libraries out there that you can choose from, and all of them have some amazing power and features behind them.

To start with, we are going to take a look at some of the best Python libraries that can help with deep learning. There are other languages that can help with things like machine learning and deep learning. But for most of the tasks that you want to do, especially if you are a beginner in data analysis and all of the processes that we have been talking about, then Python is going to be the choice for you. Even within Python, there are a number of libraries that you can choose from to get your deep learning work done. So, with that in mind, let's dive right in and see some of the best Python deep learning libraries that you can use for your data analysis

Caffe

It is pretty hard to get started with a look at deep learning libraries through Python without spending some time talking about the Caffe library. In fact, it is likely that if you have done any research on deep learning at all, then you have heard about Caffe and what it can do for some of the projects and models that you want to create.

While Caffe is technically not going to be a Python library, it is going to provide us with some bindings into the Python language. We are going to use these bindings when it is time to deploy the network in the wild, rather than just when we try to train the model. The reason that we are going to include it in this chapter is that it is used pretty much everywhere and on all of the parts of a deep learning model that you need to create.

Theano

The next kind of library that we are able to work with is known as Theano. This one has helped to develop and work with a lot of the other deep learning libraries that we have that work with Python. In the same way that a programmer would not be able to have some options like scikit-image, scikit-learn, and SciPy without NumPy, the same thing can be said when we talk about Theano and some of the other higher-level abstractions and libraries that come with deep learning.

When we take a look at the core of this, Theano is going to be one of the Python libraries that not only helps out with deep learning, but can be used to define, optimize, and evaluate a lot of mathematical expressions that will involve multi-dimensional arrays. Theano is going to accomplish this because it is tightly integrated with the NumPy library, and it keeps its use of GPU pretty transparent overall.

While you are able to use the Theano library to help build up some deep learning networks, this one is often seen as the building blocks of these neural networks, just like how the NumPy library is going to serve as the building blocks when we work on scientific computing. In fact, most of the other libraries that we will talk about as we progress through all of this are going to wrap around the Theano library, which really makes it more accessible and convenient than some of the other options.

TensorFlow

Similar to what we are able to find with the Theano library, TensorFlow is going to be an option that is open-sourced and can work with numerical computation with the help of a data flow graph. This one was originally developed to be used with research on the Google Brain Team within Google's Machine Intelligence organization. And this library, since that time, has turned into an open-sourced option so that the general public can use it for their deep learning and data science needs.

One of the biggest benefits that we are going to see with the TensorFlow library, compared to what we see with Theano, is that it is able to work with distributed computing. This is particularly true when we look at multiple-GPUs for our project, though Theano is working on improving this one as well.

Keras

Many programmers find that they love working with the Keras library when it comes to performing models and other tasks with deep learning. Keras is seen as a modular neural network library that is more minimalistic than some of the others that we talk about. This one is able to use either TensorFlow or Theano as the backend so you can choose the one that works the best for any needs you have. The primary goal that comes with this library is that you should be able to experiment on your models quickly and get from the idea that you have over to the result as fast as possible.

Many programmers like this library because the networks that you architect are going to feel almost natural and really easy, even as a beginner. It is going to include some of the best algorithms out there for optimizers, normalization, and even activation layers so this is a great one to use if your process includes these.

In addition, if you want to spend some time developing your own CNNs, then Keras is a great option to work with. Keras is set up to place a heavy focus on these kinds of neural networks, which can be valuable when you are working from the perspective of computer vision. Keras also allows us to construct both sequence-based networks, which means that the input is going to be able to flow linearly throughout that network and the graph-based network, which is where the inputs are able to skip over some of the layers if needed, only to be concatenated at a later point. This is going to make it easier for us to implement network architectures that are more complex.

One thing to note about this Python library is that it is not going to support some of the multi-GPU environments if you would like to train a network in parallel. If this is something that you want to do, then you may need to choose another library that you want to use. But for some of the work that you want to do, this may not be a big issue.

If you want to get your network trained as fast as possible, working with a library like MXNet may be a better choice. But if you are looking to tune your hyperparameters, then you may want to work with the capability of Keras to set up four independent experiments and then evaluate how the results are similar or different between each of these.

Sklearn-Theano

There are going to be times when working with deep learning when you will want to train a CNN end-to-end. And then there are times when this is not needed. Instead, when this is not needed, you can treat your CNN as the feature extractor. This is going to be the most useful with some situations you may encounter where there is just not enough data to train the CNN from scratch. So, with this one, just pass your input images through a popular pre-trained architecture that can include some options like VGGNet, AlexNet, and OverFeat. You can then use these pre-trained options and extract features from the layer that you want, usually the FC layers.

To sum this up, this is exactly what you want to have happen when you bring out this kind of library. You are not able to train a model from scratch with it so if this is your goal, then you will need to look for some other library to focus on. However, it is one of the best options to choose when you want a library that can evaluate whether a particular problem is going to be suitable for deep learning and other processes.

Nolearn

A good library for you to work with is the nolearn library. This is a good one to help out with some initial GPU experiments, especially with a MacBook Pro. It is also a good library to help out with performing some deep learning on an Amazon EC2 GPU instance.

While Keras wraps TensorFlow and Theano into a more user-friendly API, you will find that the nolearn library will be able to do the same, but it will do this with the Lasagna library. In addition, all of the code that we find with nolearn is going to be compatible with Scikit-Learn, which is a big bonus for a lot of the projects that you want to work with.

Digits

The first thing to notice with this library is that it isn't considered a true deep learning library. Although it is written out in Python and it stands for Deep Learning GPU Training System. The reason for this is because this library is more of a web application that can be used for training some of the models of deep learning that you create with the help of Caffe. You could work with the source code a bit to work with a backend other than Caffe, but this is a lot of extra work in the process. And since the Caffe library is pretty good at what it does, and can help with a lot of the deep learning tasks that you want to accomplish, it is really not worth your time.

If you have ever spent some time working with the Caffe library in the past, you can already attest to the fact that it is tedious to define your .prototxt files, generate the set of data for the image, run the network, and babysit the network training with the terminal that you are provided. The good news here is that the DIGITS library aims to fix all of this by allowing you to complete a lot of these tasks, if not all of these tasks, just from your browser. So, it may not be a deep learning library per se, but it does come into use when you struggle with the Caffe library.

In addition to all of the benefits above, the interface that the user gets to interact with is seen as excellent. This is due to the fact that it can provide us with some valuable statistics and graphs to help you rain your model more effectively. You can also easily visualize some of the activation layers of the network to help with various inputs as needed.

And finally, another benefit that is possible with this library is that if you come in with a specific image that you want to test, you have a few options on how to get this done. The first choice is to upload the image over to the DIGITS server, or you can enter in the URL that comes with the image, and then the model you make with Caffe will automatically be able to classify the image and display the results that you want in the browser.

Python is one of the best coding languages available for helping with tasks like deep learning, machine learning, and even with the topic of artificial intelligence, which encompasses both of the other two ideas. There are other languages that can handle the deep learning that we have been talking about, but none are going to be as effective, as powerful, have as many options, or be designed for a beginner in the way that Python can.

And this is exactly why we have focused our attention on the Python language and some of the best libraries that we are able to choose to help with a variety of deep learning tasks. Each of these libraries can come on board with your project and will provide us with a unique set of functions and skills to get the job done. Take a look through some of these libraries and see which one is going to be just right for your data analysis and for providing you with great insights while completing deep learning.

Chapter 4:

The Mathematics That Come with Neural Networks

T he next topic that we need to spend some time looking through is the idea of neural networks. You will not get very far with your work in deep learning if you are not able to work with these neural networks, and there are a few different types that you can create and work with as well. So, let's dive right in and learn more about these great neural networks that can help us with our deep learning models.

Neural Networks

The first type of network we are going to look at is the "normal" type of neural network. These neural networks are going to fit into the category of unsupervised machine learning because they are able to work on their own and provide us with some great results in the process. Neural networks are a great option to work within machine learning because they are set up to catch onto any pattern or trend that is found in a set of data. This can be done through a variety of levels, and in a way that is going to be much faster and more effective than a human going through and doing the work manually.

When we work with a neural network, each of the layers that we will focus on are responsible for spending time in that layer, seeing if they are able to find a pattern or trend inside the image, or through the data, that it looks at. Once it has found a trend or a pattern, it is going to start its process for entering into the next layer. This process is going to continue, with the network finding a new pattern or trend, and then going on to the next level, until it reaches a place where there are no more trends or patterns to find.

This process can end up with a lot of different layers, one over the top of the others again and again, until you have been able to see the whole thing that comes in the image. When the algorithm is created, and the program can make a good prediction based on what is in the image or in the data that you present, then you know that it has all been set up properly.

Before we move on though, we have to remember that there are a few parts that will start to occur at this point, based on how you set up the program to work. If the algorithm was able to read through all of the layers and the steps above, and it had success with reading through the different layers, then it is able to make a good prediction for you. If the algorithm is accurate with the prediction that it made, then the neurons that come with this algorithm will strengthen and become faster and more efficient at their job overall.

The reason that this happens is because the program is relying on artificial intelligence, and more specifically on deep learning, in order to create those strong associations between the patterns it saw and the object. Keep in mind that the more times that the algorithm is able to provide the right answer during this process, the more efficient it will become when you try to use it another time as well. The neurons get stronger, and you will see that the answers come faster and are more accurate overall.

Now, if you haven't been able to work with machine learning and deep learning in the past, it may seem like these neural networks would be impossible to actually see happen. But a closer examination of these algorithms can help us to see better how they work and why they can be so important to this process. For the example that we are going to work with, let's say that we have a goal to make a program that can take the image we present, and then, by going through the different layers, the program is able to recognize that the image in that picture is actually a car.

If we have created the neural network in the proper manner, then it is able to take a look at the image that we use and make a good prediction that it sees a car in the picture. The program will then be able to come up with this prediction based on any features and parts that it already knows comes with a car. This could include things like the color, the license plate, the door placement, where the headlights are, and more.

When we take a look at coding with some of the traditional methods, whether they are Python methods or not, this is something that you may be able to do, but it takes way too long and is not the best option to work with. It can take a lot of coding and really just confuse up the whole process. But with these neural networks, you will be able to write out the codes to get this kind of network done in no time.

To get the neural network algorithm to work the way that you want, you have to provide the system with a good and clear image of a car. The network can then take a look at that picture and start going through some of the layers that it needs to work with to see the picture. So, the system will be able to go through the first layer, which may include something like the outside edges of the car. When it was done with this, the network would continue on from one layer to the next, going through however many layers it takes to complete the process and provide us with a good prediction.

Sometimes this is just a few layers, but the more layers this program can go through, the more likely it will provide an accurate prediction in the end.

Depending on the situation or the project that you want to work with, there is the potential for adding in many different layers. The good news with this one is that the more details and the more layers that a neural network can find, the more accurately it can predict what object is in front of it, and even what kind of car it is looking at.

As the neural network goes through this process, and it shows a result that is accurate when identifying the car model, it is actually able to learn from that lesson, similar to what we see with the human brain. The neural network is set up in a way to remember the patterns and the different characteristics that it saw in the car model, and con store onto that information to use at another time if it encounters another car that is the same again. So, if you present, at a later time, another image with that same car model in it, then the neural network can make a prediction on that image fairly quickly.

There are several options that you can choose to use this kind of system for, but remember that each time you make a neural network, it is only able to handle one task at a time. you can make a neural network that handles facial recognition for example, and one that can find pictures that we need in a search engine, but you can't make one neural network do all of the tasks that you want. You may have to split it up and make a few networks to see this happen.

For example, there is often a lot of use for neural networks when it comes to creating software that can recognize faces. All of the information that you need to create this kind of network would not be available ahead of time, so the neural network will be able to learn along the way and get better with recognizing the faces that it sees in video or images. This is also a method that can be effective when you would like to get it to recognize different animals or recognize a specific item in other images or videos as well.

To help us out here, we need to take a look at some of the advantages that can come with this kind of model with machine learning. One of the advantages that a lot of programmers like with this one is that you can work with this algorithm without having to be in total control over the statistics of the algorithm. Even if you are not working with statistics all of the time, or you are not really familiar with how to use them, you will see that these networks can be used without those statistics, still that if there is any relationship, no matter how complex it is, is inside the information, then it is going to show up when you run the network.

The nice thing with this one is that the relationships inside your data can be found, whether the variables are dependent or independent, and even if you are working with variables that do not follow a linear path. This is great news for those who are just getting started with machine learning because it ensures that we can get a better understanding of how the data relates to each other, and some of the insights that you want to work with, no matter what variables you are working with.

With this in mind, we have to remember that there are still times when we will not use a neural network, and it will not be the solution to every problem that we want to handle in deep learning. One of the bigger issues that come with these neural network algorithms, and why some programmers decide to not use this is that the computing costs are going to be kind of high.

This is an algorithm that is pretty in-depth, and because of this, the computing costs are going to be a bit higher than what we find with some of the other options out there. and for some businesses, and even on some of the projects that you want to do with deep learning, this computation cost will just be too high. It will take on too much power, too much money, and often too much time. For some of the projects that you want to take on, the neural networks will be a great addition to your arsenal with deep learning, and other times, you may want to go another route.

Neural networks are a great option to work with when it is time to expand out your work and when you would like to create a program that can handle some more complex activities. With the right steps here, and with some time to train the neural network, you will find that the neural network is a great way to handle your data and find the trends and predictions that you want.

Recurrent Neural Networks

Now that we have had some time to look at the regular neural networks, it is time for us to dive a bit deeper and look at another option, known as the recurrent neural networks. These are going to follow some of the same rules that we can see with the discussion above, but they can also take some of your projects to the next level. Let's take a look at what these recurrent neural networks are like, and how they can really benefit a project that you are working with.

A good way to start looking at these recurrent neural networks, or RNN, is by taking a look at the human brain. When we do this, we know that it is reasonable to have the understanding that our thought processes or our understanding doesn't restart every second. We are able to retain the information that we hear and learn and then build on it. This is something that we do from childhood. We don't just see the letter A and then forget about it five seconds later. We use it as the start of the alphabet and build on that to B, C and so on. We are always building on new knowledge, whether it is from our childhood, or if it is something that we just learned.

As we go through some of the other parts that show up in this guidebook, you will start to see how each of the words, based on how much understanding you had of the words that we wrote on the page before. Your brain is not going to see a word and then immediately threw it away, and then restart its thinking process from the beginning. The point here is that our thoughts are basically able to have some consistency and some persistence with them, which is part of what makes them so powerful to work with.

With the traditional neural network that we discussed in the last section isn't capable of doing this kind of thing. And this can be a bigger shortcoming in many cases. For example, if you are working on a project that needs to classify the kind of event that is happening during all of the different parts of a movie, it wouldn't help you much with a traditional neural network because it would not be able to reason with the events that occurred earlier on in this film. There just isn't that kind of communication or power showing up within the program.

Even though the traditional neural networks may struggle with doing this kind of task and others, the good news is that we can rely on the recurrent neural networks to help us address these problems and projects in machine learning for us. These are a type of network that comes with a loop, which is going to allow the information that it learns to persist. In this method, the loop will allow information to pass from one part of the network and then move it over to the next part of the code. The recurrent neural network can be a similar idea to having multiple copies of the same network, and with each message being handed over to the successor in the process.

This chain-like nature that comes with this network is going to reveal how these networks can be intimately related to sequences and lists as we go through the process. These are going to be the natural architecture of a neural network to use for all of this data. And there are quite a few times in deep learning when these networks are going to be used.

In fact, over the past few years or so, there has already been a lot of success when it comes to applying these recurrent neural networks to a variety of projects, and it is likely that this kind of success is going to continue in the future. Some of the current examples of how the recurrent neural network can be used include speech recognition, language modeling, translation, and image captioning projects.

One of the limitations that is pretty obvious when it comes to working on these neural networks is that the API that comes with it is going to contain a good deal of constraints along the way. The API is only able to take in a vector that is a fixed size for the input, and then they can only produce a vector of a fixed size for the output, which can be a hassle when you need to take on larger forms of data to get some results.

Of course, this is just one of the issues that can come up with a system that is as complicated as an RNN. These models, for example, are able to perform the mapping that you need with a fixed number of computational steps, which is basically going to equal out to the same number as the layers that you will use to see the model.

Now, one thing to remember here is that the main reason that the RNN option is able to make your coding more exciting and can add in more work to what you can do is due to the fact that it allows the programmer to take their work and operate it over a sequence of vectors. This can often include the sequences in the input, the output, and often it will include a combination of both.

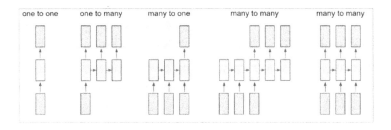

Let's take a look at the chart above. Each of the rectangles that are there is going to be a vector and the arrows are going to show us the functions. The input vectors are going to show up in red, and then the output vectors that we need to know are going to be in blue. And then the green vectors will hold onto the RNN state (which we are going to talk about in a minute). Going from the leftover to the right, let's take a look at how each of these work:

1. The first one is going to be the vanilla mode of processing, the one that doesn't use the RNN at all. This is going to include an input that is fixed and an output that is fixed. This is also known as image classification.

2. The sequence output is going to be the second part. This is going to be image captioning that is able to take an image and then will provide you with an output of a sentence of words.

3. Sequence input: This is going to be the third picture above. It is going to be more of a sentiment analysis

that shows us a given sentence and makes sure that it is classified as either a negative or positive sentiment.

4. Sequence output and sequence output. You can find this one in the fourth box, and it is getting a bit closer to what we want. This one is going to be similar to a machine translation. This is when the RNN is able to read a sentence out in English, and then can take that information and provide you with an output that reads the sentence in French.

5. And finally, the last box is going to be the synced sequence input and output. The video classification here is going to help us to label out each of the frames that occur in a video if we decide to.

Notice that in each of these, there aren't going to be any constraints put on the lengths of the sequences that we have to specify ahead of time. this is because the recurrent transformation, which is going to be shown in green, is fixed, and we are able to apply it out as many times as we would like, or as many times as work with our project.

These neural networks are a great addition to any of the codes that you would like to write out in the Python language, and they are definitely good examples of what we are able to work with when it comes to deep learning. Deep learning can lead us to a lot of different projects, many of which we may not think were possible in the past. But with some great neural networks, including the recurrent networks and the traditional neural networks, we are able to make these programs happen, search through a lot of information, and get the predictions and insights that we are looking for out of that data.

Chapter 5:

The Basics of Using Our TensorFlow Library for Deep Learning

A s we talked about a bit before, there are a lot of different libraries and options that you are able to work with when it comes to Python helping out deep learning. We talked about a few of these before, but now it is time for us to dive right into some of the best Python libraries that work with deep learning, and see how they work and what they are able to offer to you.

The first library that we are going to take a look at here is known as TensorFlow. This one needs some time because the complexities of what you can do with this library can make it a bit intimidating for a lot of people to work within the beginning. But it is a great library to go with to help with things like linear algebra and vector calculus to name a few. The Tensors that show up in this library are able to provide us with some multi-dimensional data arrays, but some more introduction is most likely needed before we dive in and really understand what these tensors are all about. So, let's get started:

TensorFlow is a type of framework that is going to come to us from Google and it is used when you are ready to create some of your deep learning models. This TensorFlow is going to rely on data-flow graphs for numerical computation. And it has been able to stop in and make machine learning easier than ever before.

It makes the process of acquiring the data, training some of the models of machine learning that you want to use, making predictions, and even modifying some of the future results that you see easier. Since all of these are important when it comes to machine learning, it is important to learn how to use TensorFlow.

This is a library that was developed by Google's Brain team to use on machine learning when you are doing it on a large scale. TensorFlow is going to bring together machine learning and deep learning algorithms and models and it makes them much more useful via a common metaphor. TensorFlow is going to use Python, just like what we say before, and it gives its users a front-end API that can be used when you would like to building applications, with the application being executed to a high-performance C++.

We will find that TensorFlow is often the library that is used when we want to not only build-up but also train and run our deep neural networks. These neural networks can be great when we want to work with image recognition, handwritten digit classification, natural language processing, recurrent neural networks, and so much more in the process. There is a lot that we are able to do with the TensorFlow language, and when it is combined together with some of the extensions, the deep learning that you can accomplish will be amazing.

TensorFlow, along with some of the other deep learning libraries that are out there, are a great option to get some of your work done. Whether you want to work with deep neural networks or another form of deep learning to help get through your data and help you find the insights and predictions that are found inside, or you are looking to find some other uses of deep learning to help your business out, TensorFlow is one of the best Python libraries out there to help you get the work done.

Plane Vectors

To start off our discussion, we need to take a look at something called a vector. The vectors in TensorFlow are going to be a special type of matrix, one that can hold onto a rectangular array of numbers to help with deep learning.

Because these vectors are going to be ordered collections of numbers, they will be seen in the view of column matrices. These vectors are going to come with one column in most cases, along with the rows that you need to get the process done. A good way to think about these vectors is a kind of scalar magnitude that is given some direction on how to behave.

Remember a good example of a scalar is going to be something like 60 m/s or 5 meters, while the vector would be more like 5 meters north. The difference that shows up between these two is that the vector will give us a direction on where to go, not just the distance, but the scalar is not going to do this and just focuses on the distance. Despite this happening, these examples are still going to be a bit different than what you may see with some of the other machine learning and deep learning projects we have focused on along the way, and this is pretty normal for now.

But, keep in mind with this one that the direction we are given in the vector is just going to be relative. This means that the direction has to be measured relative to some reference point that you add to the whole thing. We will show this direction in units of radians or in degrees to make this easier. For this one to work in most situations, you have to assume that the direction is going to be positive and that it is going to head in a rotation that is counterclockwise from the direction that we used as the reference point.

When we look at this through a more visual lens though, we have to make sure that the vectors are represented with arrows. This means that you have to consider these vectors as arrows that are going to come with a length and a direction at the same time. the direction you will need to follow can be indicated by looking at the head of the arrow, but then the length or the distance that we want to follow is going to be best indicated when we see how long the arrow truly is.

So, this is going to bring us to a crossroads where we need to focus on what these plane vectors are all about? Plane vectors are going to be a very easy setup when it comes to the tensors. They can be similar to what we see with the regular vectors that we talked about before, but the sole difference is that they are going to be found in what is known as the vector space with these ones.

This may be a bit confusing at first, but to give us a better understanding of what this means, we need to bring out an example of how it all works. Let's say in this example that we are working with a vector that is 2 X 1. This means that the vector is going to belong to a set of real numbers that are paired two at a time. To say this in another manner that may be easier to explain, they are going to both be a part of the two-space. When this does happen, you can then represent the vectors on the coordinate, with the idea of x and y like we are familiar with, plane, with rays or the arrows like we discussed.

As we work form the coordinate plane that we just discussed, we have to start out with the vectors on the standard position with an endpoint at the origin, which is the point (0, 0), or you will derive the value of our x coordinate by looking at the first row of the vector. It is also possible for us to go through at this time and find they coordinate in our second row.

The thing that we have to keep in mind with this one is that the standard position is not something that has to stay the same all of the time, and it is not something that we have to maintain either. The vectors can move, often going parallel to themselves in the same plane, and we won't have to be concerned about any of the changes that show up with this.

The Basics of the TensorFlow Library

With some of this background information ready to go and a better understanding of the tensors and vectors that come with this library, it is now time to go on another track a bit and learn some more of the basics that come with TensorFlow. We are going to start by looking at some of the steps to set up this library and get it ready to use, starting with some basics so you can become more familiar with the basics.

When you write out some of the codes that you want to use with TensorFlow, all of this is going to happen in the program this library provides, and we need to make sure that it is run as a chunk. This can seem a bit contradictory in the beginning, since we want to make sure that the programs we write out are done in Python. However, if you are able to, or if you find that this method is easier, working with the part known as the TensorFlow's Interaction Session is often the best choice. This is even a good one that helps us to be more interactive with our code writing and works well with IPython.

For what we are looking at here with some of the basics, we want to put some of our focus on the second option. This is important because it is going to help us get a nice start with not only working in the TensorFlow library but also some help with how to work with deep learning in the process. Before we get into some of the cool things that we are able to do with TensorFlow and deep learning, which we will discuss in the next section, we first need to get into a few topics to help us out.

To do any of the basics, we need to first import the TensorFlow library under the alias of "TF," as we did before. We will then be able to initialize two variables that are going to be constants. Then you need to pass an array of four numbers using the function of "constant()."

It is possible that you could go through and pass in an integer if you would like. But for the most part, working with and trying to pass an array is going to be easier and will work the best for your needs. Tensors are often about arrays so this is why it is better to use them.

Once you have put in the integer, or more likely the array, that you want to use, it is time to use the function of "multiply()" to get the variables to multiply together. Store the result as the "result" variable. And last, print out the result using the function of print().

Keep in mind that if you have defined the constants in the DataCampLight code. However, there are a few other value types that you can work within this, namely known as the placeholders. These placeholders are important because they are going to be values that are unassigned and that can be initialized by the session where you choose to let it run. Like the name is giving away, the placeholder for a particular tensor that you want to work with will be fed when the session actually runs.

During this process, we can also bring in the variables. These are the options that will have a value attached to them (you get to choose the value that you would like to attach to each of the variables as you go along), and we can change them as we go along. If you would like to go through this process and double-check that no one is able to come in here later and make changes to the values as you have them in the equation, then you need to switch over to some constants. If you are not too worried about the fact that these values can change occasionally, or you would like to have the ability to go in later and make some changes to the value, then the variables are a great option to work with.

The results of the code that you are able to write up here will end up with an abstract tensor in your computational graph. Even though this may not seem like it should work all of the time in the program, the results that come with this one are not going to be calculated. It is just going to be pushed through the algorithm and helps to define the model, but there wasn't a process that ran to help us calculate the results.

Deep Learning and TensorFlow

Now that we have had some time to look at the basics that come with TensorFlow and seen some of the benefits that come with using this library, it is time to actually take a look at how we can add TensorFlow in with some of the deep learning that we have discussed in this guidebook. The way that we are going to work with this, for now, is by constructing our own architecture for a neural network. But this time, we want to make sure that we can accomplish this with the package from TensorFlow.

Just like we can do when we bring out the Keras library (we will touch on this a bit in the next chapter), we will need to create our own neural network by going through it layer by layer. If you haven't taken the chance to do this yet, make sure that you go through and import the package for "TensorFlow" into the workspace that you want to use and use the conventional alias of "TF" to make it easier. You can also choose out another name if needed.

From this step, our goal is to initialize the graph using the simple function of Graph() to help get this done. This is an important function to bring into the group because it is the one that you will use to define the computation as you go along. Remember as we are doing the work here and we create a graph, that we do not need to worry about computing things at this time. This is due to the fact that the graph, right now at least, is not holding onto any of the values that we need. Right now, the graph is being used to define the operations that we would like to get running later.

In this situation, we are going to work with a function called as_default() to make sure that the default context is set up and ready to go. This one works the best because it will return to us a context manager that can make the specific graph that we want into the default graph. This is a good method to learn because you are able to use it any time that your model needs to have more than one graph in the same process.

When you use the function that we listed out above, you will then need to come up with what is known as the global default graph. This is important because it is the graph that will hold onto all of your operations. That is, until you go through and create a new graph to help out with this.

Once we are to this point, we also need to take some time to add in the various operations that we would like to see in the graph. The way that we do this is by building up the model. Once this is done, we compile the model and then define the metric, the optimizer, and the loss function. You can then work with TensorFlow and this is the step where we bring this in. Some of the steps that need to happen when we get to this point include:

1. Define the placeholders that you want to use for your labels and inputs because we are not going to put in the real data at this time. remember that the placeholders

that you are using here are values that are unassigned and that will be initialized as soon you as go through and run it. so, when you are ready to run the session, these placeholders are going to get the values from your set of data that you pass through in the function for run().

2. Now we want to work to build up our network. You can start this by flattening out the input, and this is done by working with the function flatten(). This will give you an array of shape, rather than the shape that is used with images that are grayscale.

3. After you have been able to flatten up the input, your construct needs to become a fully connected layer that generates logits of size. Logits is going to be the function that operates on the unscaled output of previous layers. And then it is going to use the relative scale to make sure that there is an understanding that the units are linear.

4. After you have had some time to work with the perceptron that is multi-layer, you will then be able to make sure that the loss function is defined. The choice that you make with your loss function is going to depend on what kind of task you are doing at the time.

   a. Remember here that when you use regression, it is going to be able to predict values that are continuous. When you work with classification, you are going to predict the discrete classes or values of data points.

b. From here, you can wrap up the reduce_mean) function, which is going to compute out the mean of elements across the whole tensor.

5. Now you want to take the training optimizer and define that. Some of the best algorithms that you can use to optimize this include RMSprop, ADAM, and Stochastic Gradient Descent. Depending on the algorithm you use, you may need to set up some time parameters, such as learning rate or momentum.

6. And to finish, you will need to initialize the operations in order to execute the whole thing before you go and start on the training.

While we did spend some time looking at some of the amazing things that we are able to do with the TensorFlow library, remember that these are just a sampling of all the neat models and algorithms that come with this library. This is really a great program to use because it helps you out with artificial intelligence, deep learning, and machine learning all wrapped up in one. If this sounds like a library that can help out with some of the projects that you want to complete, take some time to download it to your computer, and experiment a bit to see what deep learning models and features it is able to help you out with.

Chapter 6:

Can I Work with the Keras Library?

The next library on the list that we can focus on a bit is the Keras library. This is going to be one of the best options that we can work with when it comes to deep learning and handling all of that data you want to work with while completing a data analysis. Keep in mind here that the two top numerical platforms that we can find with Python, the ones that can provide us with some of the basis that we need for research and development in Deep learning are going to include TensorFlow and Theano.

Both of those two libraries are going to have a lot of power with them, but there are some times when they can be difficult to use in a direct manner in order to create the deep learning models that we want. Because of this, we often need to bring in the Keras library to help handle some of these models. It works on top of the TensorFlow and Theano library, so you still get the power and functionality that comes with these, with some added power and ease of use with Keras to work with deep learning.

What Is Keras?

To start, we need to take a look at some of the basics of the Keras library, what it can do for us, and the importance of learning some of this library. Keras is considered a minimalist Python library for deep learning that can run along with TensorFlow and Theano. This was a library that was developed to make implementing the models by deep learning as fast and as easy as possible, ensuring that developers and researchers are able to get things done without all of the hassle.

To use this library, the programmer needs to make sure that they have either Python 2.7 or 3.5 available on their computer. The library is also a great one because it can seamlessly execute on CPUs and GPUs given the frameworks that are underlying it. And it has been released thanks to the permissive license of MIT so that other programmers and data scientists are able to get the full benefit of using this.

The Keras library was developed and continues to be maintained by Francois Chollet, who was an engineer for Google. This library is run on the four guiding principles that include:

1. Modularity: This one goes by the idea that a model can be understood as either a graph alone or a sequence.

All of the concerns that come with the model of deep learning are going to be discrete components that the programmer can come in and combine in arbitrary ways.

2. Minimalism: This library is about cutting down on some of the clutter and keeping things as simple as possible. We find that the Keras library is going to provide us with just enough tools and functions and features to achieve our outcome. The idea is on minimal frills and maximizing the readability.

3. Extensibility: This one means that the library is set up on purpose so that it is easy to add and then use some of the new components within that framework. This was done so that researchers are able to try out new things and explore some of the new ideas that come their way without issues.

4. Python. Everything that we do in this language is going to rely on the native Python language. There will be no separate model files with custom file formats. These can be nice in some cases, but often they add in a lot of hassle and confusion that is just not worth it. Having everything work with the Python language can make a big difference.

There are so many benefits that come with working on the Keras library. It was designed to be as simple as possible while making the creation of models of deep learning a bit easier than what we can see with TensorFlow or Theano. Adding it in when you want to create some of your models can really make things easier.

We can also spend some time looking at the basics of installing this library on your system. Without installing this in the proper manner, it is going to be impossible to get all of the efficiency, and all of the model creation functionality, that we want out of this whole library.

First, we need to make sure that the Python library is all set up on our system, but we are going to assume that this is already done and move on to some of the other steps that you need to take in order to make this library work for your needs. Some of the steps that a data scientist or a programmer can use in order to add the Keras library on their system, and then start using it for their needs includes:

1. OpenCV Installation Guides. This is going to be a kind of launchpad that can link to a variety of tutorials that help with the whole installing process. This can work on any of the systems that you are trying to install this library.

2. Install Keras with TensorFlow: You will be able to use a pip in order to install both the TensorFlow and the Keras libraries in just a few minutes.

3. You can install these with the Raspberry Pi program if you would like, but this is often hard to do it on these because of the limited space, and they are hard to train ahead of time.

4. Install the libraries of Matplotlib, Scikit-Learn, and imutils. You want to make sure that these are installed on your chosen computer first. If you can, try to get this installed onto the virtual environment as well. It is easy to install these using the pip and the following code:

```
2 $ workon <your_env_name> # optional
3 $ pip install --upgrade imutils
4 $ pip install --upgrade scikit-learn
  $ pip install --upgrade matplotlib
```

With the code that we just wrote above, it is not possible to get the whole program of Keras on your computer, including all of the files and everything else that you need, in order to work with this library. It is now time to try out this library a bit and see what is inside, and how you can benefit from using this library for your own needs.

Keras and TensorFlow

While we are on this topic, we need to take a look at how Keras works with the TensorFlow library. Given that the project for TensorFlow has adopted Keras as a high-level API for the newest release it seems that this library is going to be a winner. This is because so many people are going to work with Keras along with the TensorFlow library, that the developers of TensorFlow have seen it as one library that they should welcome.

Remember that Keras is not a library that we are able to work on all on its own. It needs to have either Theano or TensorFlow behind it to finish some of the different things that we want, and to ensure that we are able to create the models of deep learning that are necessary.

While some developers like to work with Theano to get some of this work done, others like to be able to pull up TensorFlow and this is often the choice that people prefer out of all of them. All of the features that come with TensorFlow encourages it to be one of the best out there, and when you can combine it with Keras, there is nothing you can't do with deep learning.

The Principles of Keras

The principles that come with Keras are really unique and are part of the reason why this kind of Python library is going to be so great to work with, even when it comes to neural networks and deep learning models. To start with, Keras was created in order to be more user-friendly, easy to extend when needed, works with Python, and modular.

One of the key benefits that comes with this library is that it is designed for humans to use, rather than machines. Sometimes the API of some of the other coding libraries that we have talked about are too difficult to work with. They are designed without the user in mind, and learning how to bring out the functionalities and all of the algorithms can be a pain. But, with the API that is found in Keras, that is not as big of a problem. It was designed to be used for humans, while also following some of the best practices in the industry for reducing the cognitive load.

If you have taken a look at some of the other Python libraries for deep learning models before, you may have worried that the program would be too hard to work with. And this is just not the case. Keras is set up to be easy for anyone to use, and just by snooping around inside of it for a bit of time, you will notice that it is intuitive, and easy to use, no matter how complicated your model will turn out to be.

There are also a lot of standalone modules that come with the Keras library. You will be able to combine these together as needed to create the new models that you need with Python behind them. Some of the examples of the standalone modules that you can enjoy will include the regularization schemes, activation functions, initialization schemes, optimizers, cost functions, and neural layers to name a few.

In addition to combining some of these standalone modules to create some of the new models that you want to work with, it is easy to add in new modules. This is usually done as new functions or classes. The models that are done here will be defined in the code of Python, rather than having their own separate model configuration files to work with.

The biggest reasons that you and other programmers would want to work with the Keras library stem from those guiding principles that we talked about before. Primarily, the fact that Keras is so user-friendly is making big waves in this industry. Beyond the ease of learning this, and how easy it makes the process of building models, Keras is going to offer us the advantages of broad adoption, a support for a lot of options of production deployment, integration with a minimum of five engines for the backend, and a strong support for a lot of

GPUs. We even find that it can help out with some of the distributed training that we need to complete.

If you are still uncertain that this is the right library for you, think about all of the companies who are already working with this library. It is not just programmers and a few researchers who are happy with this library and using it for their own needs, but also some of the big names in companies out there are using this library as well. These include Uber, NVIDIA, Apple, Amazon, Microsoft, and Google.

Building a Deep Learning Model with Keras

The final thing that we need to take a look at here is how we are able to work with the Keras library in order to help us build some of our own models of deep learning. The focus on Keras is going to be the idea of a model. The main model that we are able to work within this library is going to be known as a Sequence, and this is a linear stack of layers.

As a programmer, you will start out with a basic sequence, and then you can add in some layers to it, adding them in the order that you wish for them to be computed during the execution. Once you have had some time to define these, you can then compile the model you will use, which basically will make sure of the underlying framework to optimize the computation that you want to see performed by that model. During this time, the programmer or the researcher is able to specify the loss function, and the optimizer, that they want to use.

After we have had some time to go through and compile all of this information, we need to then take the model and find a method to fit it to the data. There are a few methods that we are able to use to get this done. First, you can do the fitting one batch of data at a time, or you can do it by firing off the entire regime for the model training. This is where we will see the computing happen in the first place.

Now, the training process is going to take some time, and it may not be as efficient as we may hope. But the more data that we can show to the model, and the more time we take to get this done with some high-quality data, the better the model is going to perform. Once the model is properly trained, you can then use that model to look through new data presented and make some good predictions for you.

While there are a number of steps that have to happen to turn the model into something that you can use for insights and predictions, especially when it is a deep learning model, we are able to summarize this to make things a bit easier. The summary that is needed to help us explain the construction of deep learning models in Keras will include the following steps:

1. Define the model. This means that we have to start out with creating our own sequence and then adding in the number of layers that we want to work with.

2. Compile the model. This is the step where the programmer or the researcher is able to specify all of the optimizers, as well as the loss functions.

3. Fit your model. This is the step where you are able to execute the model with all of the data that has been collected. This is going to include a lot of training to ensure that the model is going to work the way that we want.

4. Make predictions. After the model has had the time to go through the proper training, we are then able to use that model to help generate some of the predictions that are needed on any new data that is presented. The model will get faster and more efficient at the predictions as time goes on and it receives more data and more feedback.

There is so much to love when it comes to working with the Keras library. Many people worry that it is going to be too hard to work with, or that they shouldn't waste their time because this library won't add in any functionalities or extras that we can't get from Theano or TensorFlow. However, this is a library that is able to stand on its own. While it does rely on one or the other of those libraries above, it can make deep learning model creation easier and will ensure that we are able to see the best results with some of our models in no time.

Chapter 7:

The PyTorch Library and How This Method Can Help with Machine Learning

The next library that we need to take a look at is known as PyTorch. This is going to be a Python-based package that works for scientific computing that is going to rely on the power that it can receive from graphics processing units. This library is also going to be one of the most common, and the preferred, deep learning platforms for research in order to provide us with maximum flexibility and a lot of speed in the process.

There are a lot of benefits that come with this kind of library. And it is known for providing two of the most high-level features out of all the other deep learning libraries. These will include tensor computation with the support of a strong GPU acceleration, along with being able to build up the deep neural networks on an autograd-system that is tape-based.

There are a lot of different libraries through Python that can help us work with a lot of artificial intelligence and deep learning projects that we want to work with. And the PyTorch library is one of these. One of the key reasons that this library is so successful is because it is completely Pythonic and one that is able to take some of the models that you want to build with a neural network almost effortlessly. This is a newer deep learning library to work with, but there is a lot of momentum in this field as well.

The Beginnings of PyTorch

As we mentioned above, PyTorch is one of the newest libraries out there that works with Python and can help with deep learning. Even though it was just released in January 2016, it has become one of the go-to libraries that data scientists like to work with, mainly because it can make it easy to build up really complex neural networks. This is perfect for a lot of beginners who haven't been able to work with these neural networks at all in the past. They can work with PyTorch and make their own network in no time at all, even with a limited amount of coding experience.

The creators of this Python library envisioned that this library would be imperative when they wanted to run a lot of numerical computations as quickly as possible. This is one of the ideal methodologies that also fits in perfectly with the programming style that we see with Python. This library, along with the Python library, as allowed debuggers of neural networks, machine learning developers, and deep learning scientists to not only run but also to test, parts of their code in real-time. This is great news because it means that these professionals no longer have to wait for the entire code to complete and execute before they can check out whether this code works or if they need to fix certain parts.

In addition to some of the functionality that comes with the PyTorch library, remember that you are able to extend out some of the functionalities of this library by adding in other Python packages. Python packages like Cython, SciPy, and NumPy all work well with PyTorch as well.

Even with these benefits, we still may have some questions about why the PyTorch library is so special, and why we may want to use this when it is time to build up the needed models for deep learning. The answer with this is simple, mainly that PyTorch is going to be seen as a dynamic library. This means that the library is really flexible and you can use it with any requirements and changes that you would like. It is so good at doing this job that it is being used by developers in artificial intelligence, students, and researchers in many industries. In fact, in a Kaggle competition, this library was used by almost all of the individuals who finished in the top ten.

While there are a lot of benefits that can come with the PyTorch library, we need to start off with some of the highlights of why professionals of all sorts love this language so much. Some of these include:

1. The interface is simple to use. The PyTorch interface is going to offer us an API that is easy to use. This means that we will find it simple to operate and run like we do with Python.

2. It is Pythonic in nature. This library, since it is considered Pythonic, will smoothly integrate to work with the Python data science stack. For those who do not want to work with other coding languages along the way, and want to just stick with the basics, and some of the power, of Python, will be able to do so with this library. You will get the leverage of using all of the functionalities and services that are offered through the environment of Python.

3. Computational graphs: Another highlight that comes with the PyTorch library is that it is going to provide us with the platform with some dynamic computational graphs. This means that you have the ability to change these graphs up even during runtime. This is going to be useful any time that you need to work on some graphs and you are not sure how much memory you need to use while creating this model for a neural network.

The Community for PyTorch

The next thing that we need to take a look at here is some of the community that comes with the PyTorch library. Because of all the benefits that come with PyTorch, we can see that the community of developers and other professionals is growing on a daily basis. In just a few years, this library has shown a lot of developments and has even led this library to be cited in many research papers and groups. And when it comes to artificial intelligence and models of deep learning, PyTorch is starting to become one of the main libraries to work with.

One of the interesting things that come with PyTorch is that it is still in the early-release beta. But because so many programmers are adopting the framework for deep learning already, and at such a brisk pace, it already shows the power and the potential that comes with it, and how the community is likely to continue growing. For example, even though we are still on the beta release with PyTorch, there are currently 741 contributors just on the GitHub repository right now. This means that there are more than 700 people working to enhance and add some improvements to the functionalities of PyTorch that are already there.

Think of how amazing this is! PyTorch is not technically released yet and is still in the early stages. But there has been so much buzz around this deep learning library, and so many programmers have been using it for deep learning and artificial intelligence, that there are already a ton of contributors who are working to add some more functionality and improvements to this library for others to work with.

PyTorch is not going to limit the specific applications that we are working with because of the modular design and the flexibility that comes with it. It has seen a heavy amount of use by some of the leading tech giants, and you may even recognize some of the names. Those who have already started to work with PyTorch to improve their own deep learning models will include Uber, NVIDIA, Twitter, and Facebook. This library has also been used in a lot of domains for research including neural networks, image recognition, translation, and NLP among other key areas.

Why Use PyTorch with the Data Analysis

Anyone who is working with the field of data science, data analysis, artificial intelligence, or deep learning has likely spent some time working with the TensorFlow library that we also talked about in this guidebook. TensorFlow may be the most popular library from Google, but because of the PyTorch framework for deep learning, we can find that this library is able to solve a few new problems when it comes to research work that these professionals want to fix.

It is often believed that PyTorch is now the biggest competitor out there to TensorFlow when it comes to handling data, and it is going to be one of the best and most favorited artificial intelligence and deep learning library when it comes to the community of research. There are a number of reasons for this happening, and we will talk about some of these below:

First, we will notice that the dynamic computational graphs are going to be popular among researchers. This library is going to avoid some of the static graphs that can be used in other frameworks from TensorFlow. This allows researchers and developers to change up how the network is going to behave at the last minute. Some of those who are adopting this library will like it because these graphs are more intuitive to learn when we compare it to what TensorFlow is able to do.

The second benefit is that this one comes with a different kind of back-end support. PyTorch is going to use a different backend based on what you are doing. The GPU, CPU, and other functional features will all come with a different backend rather than focusing on just one back-end to handle all of these. For example, we are going to see the THC for our GPU, and TH for CPU. Being able to use separate backends can make it easier for us to deploy this library through a variety of constrained systems.

The imperative style is another benefit of working with this kind of library. This means that when we work with this library, it is easy to use and very intuitive. When you execute a line of code, it is going to get executed just as you want, and you are able to work with some tracking that is in real-time. this allows the programmer to keep track of how the models for neural networks are doing. Because of the excellent architecture that comes with this, and the lean and fast approach, it has been able to increase some of the overall adoption that we are seeing with this library throughout the communities of programmers.

Another benefit that we are going to enjoy when it comes to working with PyTorch is that it is easy to extend. This library, in particular, is integrated to work well with the code for C++ and it is going to share a bit of the backend with this language when we work on our own framework for deep learning. This means that a programmer is going to be able to not just use Python for the CPU and GPU, but it can also add in the extension of the API using the C or the C++ languages. This means that we are able to extend out the usage of PyTorch for some of the new and experimental cases, which can make it even better when we want to do some research with it.

And finally, the last benefit that we are going to focus on here is that PyTorch is going to be seen as a Python approach library. This is because the library is a native Python package just by the way that it is designed. The functionalities that come with this are built as classes in Python, which means that all of the code that you write here can integrate in a seamless manner with the modules and packages of Python.

Similar to what we see with NumPy, this Python-based library is going to enable us to work on a tensor that is GPU-accelerated, with computations that provide us with some rich options for APIs while applying a neural network. PyTorch is going to provide us with the research framework that we need from one end to another, which will come with most of the different building blocks that we need to carry out the research of deep learning on a day to day basis. And we also notice that this library is going to provide us with a high-level neural network modules because it can work with an API that is similar to the Keras library as well.

PyTorch 1.0 – How This Moves Us from Research to Production

During this chapter, we have spent some time discussing a lot of the strengths that we are able to see with the PyTorch library, and how these will help to make lots of researchers and data scientists run to it as their go-to library. However, there are a few downsides that come with this library and one of these includes that it has been really lacking when it comes to support of production. However, due to some of the improvements and changes that will happen with PyTorch, it is expected that this is something that will change soon.

The next release of PyTorch, which is known as PyTorch 10, is already expected to be a big release that is meant to overcome some of the biggest challenges that researchers, programmers, and developers face in production. This is the newest iteration of the whole framework, and it is expected to combine with the Python-based Caffe2, allowing for deep learning researchers and machine learning developers to move from research to production. And the point of doing this is to allow the process to happen in a manner that is hassle-free and without the programmer needing to deal with challenges that show up in migration.

The new version 1.0 is meant to help to unify the research and production capabilities in one framework, rather than doing it in two parts, making things easier and avoiding some of the missed values and complications that happen when you try to merge together two parts. This allows us with more performance optimization and the flexibility that we need to complete both research and production.

This newer version is going to promise us a lot of help with handling the tasks that come up. Many of these tasks are going to make it more efficient to run your models of deep learning on a much larger scale. Along with the support of production, remember that PyTorch 10 will have a lot of improvements with optimization and usability.

With the help of the PyTorch 1.0 library, we are going to be able to take the existing code and continue to work on it as-is. The existing API is not going to change so that makes it easier for those who have already been able to create some coding and programs with the old API. To help make sense of the progress that is going to happen with the PyTorch library, you can look at the PyTorch website to help out.

As we can see with all of the information that we explored in this chapter, PyTorch is already seen as a compelling player when it comes to the various processes that we can do with artificial intelligence and deep learning. Being able to exploit all of the unique parts that come with this, and seeing that it is going to work as a research first library can be an important part of our data analysis overall.

The PyTorch library is able to overcome some of the challenges that it has and can provide us with all of the power and the performance that is necessary to get the job done. If you are a student, a researcher, or a mathematician who is inclined to work with some of the models of deep learning, then the PyTorch library is going to be a great option as a framework for deep learning to help you get started.

Chapter 8:

Looking at Machine Learning and How This Fits In

W hile we are on this topic, we need to also spend some time looking at machine learning and how it is able to fit in with the topics of deep learning and our data analysis. Machine learning is another topic that is getting a lot of attention throughout the business world, no matter which industry you spend your time in, and learning how to make this happen, and the importance of machine learning and other parts of artificial intelligence in your project and the models that you create.

When you start diving into all of the advancements that are present with artificial intelligence it sometimes seems a bit overwhelming. But if you are just interested in learning some of the basics for now, you can boil down a lot of the innovations that come with artificial intelligence into two main concepts that are equally as important. These two concepts are going to include the deep learning that we have already spent some time on, and machine learning as well.

These are two terms that have garnered a lot of attention over the years, and because of the buzz that comes with them, it is likely that many business owners assume that these words can be used interchangeably. But there are some key differences that come between machine learning and deep learning, and it is definitely important to know the differences and how these two methods relate to each other

With that in mind, we are going to take some time to explore more about machine learning and how it is able to fit into the model that we are creating. There are a lot of examples of both deep learning and machine learning, and we use both of these topics on a regular basis. So, let's dive right in and see a bit more about the differences and similarities between machine learning and deep learning.

What Is Machine Learning?

The first thing that we need to take a look at here is the basics of machine learning. This is going to include a lot of algorithms that are able to first parse the data we have, learn from that data, and then apply what they were able to learn from that data over to make a more informed decision. Basically, it is a process we can use in order to teach our machines and programs on how to learn and make important decisions on their own.

Let's take a look at an example of how this is meant to work. A good example of this process would be a streaming service for on-demand music. For this service to stick with some decisions about which artists or songs to recommend to one of their listeners, the algorithms of machine learning will be hard at work. These algorithms are able to associate the preferences of the user with other listeners who have a similar taste in music. This technique, which is often given the generic name of artificial intelligence, is going to be used in many of the other services that are able to offer us recommendations in an automatic manner.

Machine learning is going to fuel all sorts of tasks that are automated and that can span across many industries. This could start out with some firms for data security, who will hunt down malware and turn it off before it infects a lot of computers. And it can go to finance professionals who want to prevent fraud and make sure they are getting the alerts when there are some good trades they can rely on.

We are able to take some of the algorithms that come with artificial intelligence and program them in a manner that makes them learn on a constant basis. This is going to be done in a manner that stimulates the actions of a virtual personal assistant, and you will find that the algorithms are able to do these jobs very efficiently.

Machine learning is going to be a complex program to work with, and often it takes the right coding language, such as Python, and some of the best libraries out there to get things done. The algorithms that you can create will involve a lot of complex coding and math that can serve as a mechanical function. This function is similar to what we may see a screen on a computer, a car or a flashlight do for us.

When we say that something such as a process or a machine, is able to do "machine learning" this basically means that it's something that is able to perform a function with the data you provide over to it, and then it can also get progressively better at doing that task as time goes on. Think of this as having a flashlight that is able to turn on any time that you say the words "it is dark," so it could recognize the different phrases that have the word dark inside of them, and then knows to continue on with the action at hand.

Now, the way that we can train these machines to do the tricks above, and so much more, can be really interesting. And there is no better way to work with this than to add in a bit of neural networking and deep learning to the process to make these results even more prevalent overall.

Machine Learning Vs. Deep Learning

Now we need to take a look at how machine learning and deep learning are going to be the same, and how they can be different. When we look at this in practical terms, deep learning is simply going to be a subset that we see with machine learning. In fact, one reality that we see with this is that deep learning is technically going to be a type of machine learning, and it will function in a manner that is similar. This is why so many people who haven't been able to work with either of these topics may assume that they are the same thing. However, it is important to understand that the capabilities between deep learning and machine learning are going to be different.

While the basic models that come with machine learning are going to become steadily better what the function you are training them to work with, they are still going to rely on some guidance from you as well. If the algorithm gives you a prediction that is inaccurate, then the engineer has to step in and make sure that the necessary adjustments are done early on. With a model that relies on deep learning though, the algorithm can determine, without any help, whether the prediction that it made is accurate. This is done with the help of a neural network.

Let's go back to the example that we did with the flashlight earlier. You could program this to turn on any time that it can recognize the audible cue of someone when they repeat the word "dark." As it continues to learn, it might then turn on with any phrase that has that word as well. This can be done with just a simple model out of machine learning.

But if we decide to add in a model from deep learning to help us get this done, the flashlight would then be able to turn on with some other cues. Instead of just waiting for the word "dark" to show up, we would see it work when someone said a phrase like "the light switch won't work" or "I can't see" which shows that they are in need of a light right then. A deep learning model is going to be able to learn through its own method of computing, which is going to be a technique that helps the system act in a manner that seems like it has its own brain.

Adding in the Deep Learning to the Process

With this in mind, a model of deep learning is going to be designed in a manner that can continually analyze data with a logic structure, and this is done in a manner that is similar to the way that a human would look at problems and draw conclusions. To help make this happen, the application of deep learning is going to work with an artificial neural network, which is going to be basically a layered structure of algorithms that we can use for learning.

The design of this kind of network can seem a bit confusing in the beginning, but it is designed to work similar to the biological neural network that we see in the human brain. This is a great thing for the machine learning and deep learning that you want to do because it can lead us over to a process of learning that will be more capable of hard and complex than what the standard models with machine learning can do.

Of course, there are going to be times when it is tricky to ensure that the model of deep learning isn't going to draw some conclusions that are incorrect. We want it to be able to work on its own to get results, but we have to make sure that we are not getting the wrong answers out of the model. And we need to catch these issues as quickly as possible. If the model is able to continue on and learn the wrong outputs and information, then it is not going to be incorrect the whole time and will not do the work that we want.

Just like with some of the other examples that we are able to use with artificial intelligence, it is going to require a lot of training to make sure that we can see the learning processes turn out the right way. but when this is able to work the way that it should, the functional deep learning is going to be seen ore as a scientific marvel that can be the backbone of true artificial intelligence.

A good example that we can look at right now for deep learning is the AlphaGo product from Google. Google worked on creating a computer program that worked with a neural network. In this computer program, the network was able to learn how to play the board game that is known as Go, which is one of those games that needs a lot of intuition and intellect to complete.

This program started out by playing against other professional players of Go, the model was able to learn how to play the game and beat out some of these professionals, beating a level of intelligence in a system that had never been seen before. And all of this was done without the program being told at all when it should make a specific move. A model that followed the standard machine learning requirements would need this guidance. But this program is going to do it all on its own.

The part that really shocked everyone and brought this kind of technology to the forefront is the idea that it was able to defeat many world-renowned "masters" of the game. This means that not only could the machine learn about some of the abstract aspects and complex techniques of the game, but it was also becoming one of the best players of the game as well.

To recap this information and to help us to remember some of the differences that show up between machine learning and deep learning, we need to discuss some of the following:

1. Machine learning is going to work with algorithms in order to parse data, learn from the data it has, and then make some smart and informed decisions based on what the algorithm has been able to learn along the way.

2. The structures of deep learning algorithms are going to come in layers. This helps us to end up with an artificial neural network, that is going to learn and make some intelligent decisions all on its own.

3. On the other hand, deep learning is going to be a subfield of machine learning. Both of them are going to fall under the category of artificial intelligence. But with deep learning, we are going to see more of what powers the artificial intelligence that resembles the human way of thinking in a machine.

Now, this is all going to seem a bit complicated at times because there is just so much that has to come into play to make this work. The easiest takeaway for us to understand some of the differences between what we see with deep learning and machine learning is to just realize that deep learning is a type of machine learning.

To make this a bit further and to add in some specifics, deep learning is going to be considered a kind of evolution of machine learning, and shows us how this kind of technology has changed over the years. There are a lot of techniques that can show up with this kind of learning, but it often workings with a neural network that we can program, and that will enable a machine to make decisions that are accurate, without getting any help from a programmer.

Data Is the Fuel We Need for the Future

With all of the data that we see being produced in our current era, the era of Big Data, it is no surprise that we are going to see some innovations that marvel and surprise us all of the time. And there are likely that we will see a lot of new innovations in the future that we can't even fathom yet. According to many experts who are in the field, we will likely see a lot of these innovations show up in applications with deep learning.

This can be a great thing for our future. Think of how this kind of technology is going to be able to take over the world and help us to do things and experience things in ways that we never thought possible. And just think about where this kind of technology is going to be able to take us in the future, and how it is going to change up a lot of the way that we interact with each other and with other businesses as well.

Many of the applications that we see with artificial intelligence show up in customer service. These are going to be used to help drive the advent of self-service, they can increase the productivity of the agent, and they ensure that the workflows are more reliable.

The data that is fed into these algorithms will come from a constant flux of incoming customer queries. This can include a lot of relevant context into some of the issues that the customers of the business are facing. There is already a lot of data that a business is able to collect when they work with their customers, and they can add in some third-party surveys and even ask customers for opinions in order to create some good machine learning algorithms. These algorithms then can help us figure out what the customers want, what products to release, and more.

Machine learning and deep learning are two topics that seem to be almost the same, and for those who are just getting started with this kind of process, it is hard to see how these two terms are going to be different. as we dive more into the idea of a data analysis and what we are able to do with all the data we have been collected, we will see that machine learning and deep learning are two very different processes that can help us do some amazing.

Chapter 9:

How Deep Learning Can Help with Completing Your Own Predictive Analysis

Many times, we can all agree that machine learning has been able to step in and readily improve the way that we are going to interact with all of the data we have, and with the internet. For example, when we talk about machine learning, we can see it work with the search engines that we use, in spam filters that get rid of unwanted emails based on just snippets of the wording in each one, and even facial recognition software.

However, it is intriguing to take this a bit further and learn more about how all of this works. We are going to start out with our own model of machine learning here to see how things will work, and how we can use this for some of our own predictive analysis as we go. For this one, we want to be able to separate out the peaches from the mangoes. For machine learning to work, we have to be able to create our own digital image of the objects, and then we can classify them based on the sets of their features.

This is something that a simple handwritten code is able to do. This code needs to have some descriptions inside of it that will be able to add in inputs about the fruits including color, shape, and some of the other metrics that are involved in the segregation between the peach and the mango. Once the code is written, and it has enough power behind it, the machine will be able to extract the shape and the color out of each desired fruit.

Now, in this program, we will find that the images can be differentiated depending on the spaces as both fruits are going to be put on their own points inside that chart. This means that if at a later time you add in a new point within the map, the machine can have some success with separating out the peach and the mango, based on the characteristics that you provided for each fruit in the morning.

This is basically what the algorithms for machine learning are all about. It is there to use a lot of techniques, including deep learning, to help differentiate the data from other parts of data. And this is exactly how machine learning, and some of the techniques that come with it, can then move into the realms of things like self-learning and sometimes even artificial intelligence.

Of course, even with all of that in mind, we have to remember that machine learning, just like with any of the other options of artificial intelligence and data analysis that we want to work with, can be prone to mistakes This is especially true when you first start working with the model. Errors are often going to be experienced when we have a new set of computed features when they are closer to the existing classes that we work with.

An example of this would be if you have a mango that is not quite the right shape, and seems to resemble a peach a bit more. Or if the mango images are not in cohesion with one another when it comes to the shape. To help us minimize the errors that we see we should add in an extra layer and more classes to ensure that the algorithm is as accurate as possible.

What Is a Predictive Analysis?

One topic that we need to explore a bit while we are here, before diving into how deep learning is able to help us out with it, is what predictive analytics is all about. To keep it simple, predictive analytics is going to be the use of techniques from machine learning, data, and statistical algorithms to help identify the likelihood of future outcomes based on data that is more historical. The goal is to go beyond what we know happened in the past to provide the best predictions and guess what will happen in the future.

Though the idea of predictive analytics is something that has been around for a long time, it is a technology that is starting to garner more attention than ever. Many companies, throughout a variety of industries, are turning to predictive analytics to increase their bottom line, and to add a competitive advantage to everyone who uses it. Some of the reasons why this predictive analysis is gaining so much popularity now includes:

1. The data that is available can help with this. The growing volume as well as the types of data are a good place to start. And there is more interest from many companies in using data to help produce some great insights in the process.
2. The computers and systems that are needed to complete this predictive analysis is cheaper and faster than ever before.
3. The software to finish the predictive analysis is easier to use.
4. There is a lot of competition out there for companies to work again. Thanks to these tougher conditions in the

economy, and with the competition, businesses need to find their own way to differentiate and become better than the competition. A predictive analysis can help them to do this.

With all of the interactive software that is easier than ever to use predictive analytics has grown so much. It is no longer just the domain of those who study math and statistics. Business experts and even business analysts are able to use this kind of technology as well.

With this in mind, it is time to take a look at how the predictive analysis. Predictive models are going to work by using known results to help train or develop a model that can be used to predict values for different or new data. Modeling that comes with the predictive analysis can provide us with results, often in the form of a prediction that can represent a probability of the target variable. This variable is going to vary based on the results that you are looking to find and could include something like revenue.

Keep in mind here that this is going to be a bit different compared to the descriptive models that can help us understand what happened in the past, or some of the diagnostic models that we can use that help us understand some key relationships and determine why we say a certain situation happen in the past. In fact, there are entire books that will be devoted to the various techniques and methods that are more analytical than others. And there are even complete college curriculums that will dive into this subject as well, but we can take a look at some of the basics that come with this process and how we can use this for our needs as well.

There are two types of predictive models that we can take a look at first. These are going to include the classification models and regression models. To start with are the classification models that work to predict the membership of a class. For example, you may work on a project to try and figure out whether an employee is likely to leave the company, whether a person is going to respond to solicitation from your business, or whether the person has good or bad credit with them before you loan out some money.

For this kind of model, we are going to stick with binary options which means the results have to come in at a 0 or a 1. So, the model results will have these numbers, and 1 tells us that the event that you are targeting is likely to happen. This can be a great way to make sure that we see whether something is likely to happen or not.

Then we have the regression models. These are going to be responsible for predicting a number for us. A good example of this would be predicting how much revenue a customer is going to generate over the next year, or how many months we have before a piece of our equipment will start to fail on a machine so you can replace it.

There are a lot of different techniques that we are able to work with when it comes to predictive modeling. The three most common types of techniques that fall into this category of predictive modeling will include regression, decision trees, and neural networks. Let's take a look at some of these to see how these can all work together.

First on the list is a decision tree. These are an example of classification models that we can take a look at. This one is going to partition the data we want to work with and put it into subsets, based on categories of the variables that we use as input. A decision tree is going to look like a tree that has each branch representing one of the choices that we can make. when we set this up properly it is able to help us see how each choice we want to make compares to the alternatives. Each leaf out of this decision tree is going to represent a decision or a classification of the problem.

This model is helpful to work with because it looks at the data presented to it and then tries to find the one variable that is there that can split up the data. We want to make sure that the data is split up into logical groups that are the most different from each other.

The decision tree is going to be popular because they are easy to interpret and understand. They are also going to do well when it is time to handle missing values, and are useful when it comes to preliminary selection of your data. So, if you are working with a set of data that is missing many values or you would like a quick and easy answer that you can interpret in no time, then a decision tree is a good one to work with.

Then we need to move on to the regression. We are going to take a look at logistic and linear regression. The regression is going to be one of the most popular models to work with The regression analysis is going to estimate the relationship that is present among the variables. It is also intended for continuous data that can be assumed to follow a normal distribution, it finds any of the big patterns that are found in sets of data, and it is often going to be used to determine some of the specific factors that answer our business questions, such as the price that can influence the movement of an asset.

As we work through with the regression analysis, we want to make sure that we can predict a number, which is called the response, or in this case the Y variable. With some linear regressions, we are going to have one independent variable that can be used to help explain, or else predict, the outcome of Y. And then the multiple regression is going to work with two or more independent variables to help us predict what the outcome will be.

Then we can move on to the logistic regression. With this one, we are going to see that it is the unknown variable of a discrete variable that is predicted based on the known value of some of the variables. The response variable is going to be more categorical, which means that it can assume only a limited number of values compared to the others.

And finally, we have the binary logistic regression. This one is going to be a response variable that has only two values that go with it. All of the results that happen will come out as either 0 or as a 1. If we see 0, this means that the expected result is not going to happen. And if it shows up as a 1, then this means that our expected result is going to happen.

And then we can end with the neural networks like we talked about before. These are going to be a more sophisticated technique that we are able to work with that have the ability to model really complex relationships. These are popular for a lot of reasons, but one of the biggest reasons is that the neural networks are so flexible and powerful.

The power that we are able to see with the neural network is going to come with the ability that these have with handling nonlinear relationships in data, which is going to become more and more common as we work to collect some more data. Many times, a data scientist will choose to work with the neural network to help confirm the findings that come with the other techniques that you used, including the decision trees and regression.

The neural networks are going to be based on a lot of features including pattern recognition and some of the processes of artificial intelligence that can model our parameters in a graphical manner. These are going to work well when no mathematical formula is known that relates to both the inputs and the outputs that we are doing., when prediction is going to be more important than working with the explanation, or when there is a ton of training data that we can work with.

Another option that we have to look at is the artificial neural networks. These were originally developed by researchers who were trying to mimic what we can find in the brain of a human on a machine. And when they were successful, we get a lot of the modern pieces of technology that we like to use today.

A predictive analysis is going to do a lot of great things for your business. It can ensure that you will be able to handle some of the more complex problems that your business faces, and will make it easier to know what is likely to happen in the future. Basing your big business decisions on data, and the insights found with predictive analysis can make it easier to beat out the competition and get ahead.

Looking into Deep Learning

Now, going apart from some of the categories that we manually code, a machine is able to use some of the neural networks to help it learn the features of the objects you are working with. Looking back at the example above, we can use the neural network to help the machine learn some of the features that happen with peaches and mangoes, and the machine can do it all on itself.

Remember from before, remember that these networks are going to work in a manner that is similar to what we see with the brain, and they are going to comprise of artificial neurons to help us model the data. There is also going to be a type of synaptic response as well with the network that uses different values as the inputs. The values that come with the featured output can then be used as the new input to the other artificial neurons.

These neural networks are going to be the very core of what we see with machines that can learn on their own. And we can expect, after the right kind of training and testing, that they will segregate peaches from mangoes by learning the traits from the perceived images.

This is a great place for deep learning to come into play because it will help us to define the number of layers that we need to use inside our neural network. To make this easier, this is basically the term of the depth of a given network. For the network to be considered exhaustive, we need to add in as many layers as possible, so we need to make it as deep as we can.

Even when you have taken the time to create a neural network, and the features are all set up, many aren't going to be put in real practice. The main reason that this happens is because there isn't enough data to make the training work. If you have not been able to collect a lot of big data to use to train the model, then the model will never know how it should behave, and there is no way to ensure accuracy.

The most important pitfall that comes with this one though is that the machine, or the system, may not be able to generate enough computing power to get the work done. This is again a place where big data can come in and help. This big data is able to help deep learning and the networks in a natural manner and can offer some computational power with the help of business intelligence. If you are able to add in enough power behind what you are doing here, and you use big data in the proper manner, you will find that the issues with computational power will not be as big of an issue.

The Applications of Deep Learning

In many companies, the use of machine learning and deep learning techniques are going to be widely used. They can be used in the medical field to help us learn more about different diseases and to help a doctor provide an accurate diagnosis in a faster manner. They can be used in the retail industry to help figure out the best marketing techniques to reach customers and where to place different products. Manufacturing firms can use deep learning to help them find where waste is to eliminate it, and to make predictions on when a piece of equipment is going to fail, so they can fix it ahead of time.

Even with all of these options, there are still some other targeted approaches and uses of machine learning, especially the kind that have been assisted with deep learning. Some of these are going to include:

1. Text analysis: This is going to be a form of predictive analytics that can help us extract what the sentiments behind the text, based on the intensity of the presses on the keys, and the typing speeds.

2. Artificial intelligence: This may be its own field, but it can take a lot of its cues from deep learning. This is because many of the artificial intelligence models that you work with are going to put the idea of neural networks to use. Google DeepMind is a good example of this.

3. Predictive anomaly analysis: Deep learning can help us to find out when there are some anomalies and abnormal patterns in signals. This can be useful for many companies who want to catch catastrophes early on and can help us to avoid some failures on major systems.

   a. The deep neural networks are going to be preferred in many cases when it is time to detect these anomalies because it is able to take the input signal and reconstruct it as the output. If there are any changes that happen with the journey, this will be reported. If you have a network that goes really deep, it is possible to work with this information in a manner that is more refined.

4. Failure analysis: Neural networks are often able to detect failures that will happen, ahead of time, even when they aren't meant for the failing system. The server overloads and some other behaviors that may be erratic are also easily detected if we set up deep learning.

5. Disruptions in IT environments: Most of the organizational services of seen some big changes over the years, including things like microservices, delivery systems, and IoT's. While most teams are working on a variety of tools to help comprehend the nature of these services, deep learning is going to be helpful when it is time to gauge the patterns and then change up the IT stacks.

Deep learning, along with machine learning, is the key to the future of big data, and even to what we can see with business intelligence. This is why it is important for us to address the issues of neural networks, with as much precision as we can. The more precision that comes with these neural networks and running them, the better they will perform. And we can bet that as time goes on, machine learning is going to be the part that helps us to really handle a lot of menial and even up to complex tasks in no time.

Conclusion

T hank you for making it through to the end of *Python for Data Analysis*, let's hope it was informative and able to provide you with all of the tools you need to achieve your goals whatever they may be.

The next step is to start putting some of the models and the Python libraries that we discussed in this guidebook to good use. Companies are already gathering up large amounts of data. Now it is time for us to take this data and actually learn what predictions and insights are found inside all of this data. This guidebook took some time looking at deep learning and how it can make our data analysis easier than ever before. This data analysis is going to make a difference in how you can run your business, and it will ensure that you are able to get the best results each time out of that data. We looked at the different languages, libraries, and techniques that we can use when it comes to using deep learning for our data analysis. When you are ready to take all of that data you have collected and put it to use with a good data analysis with deep learning, make sure to check out this guidebook to help you get started. Finally, if you found this book useful in any way, a review on Amazon is always appreciated!